Communications
in Computer and Information Science   1079

Commenced Publication in 2007
Founding and Former Series Editors:
Phoebe Chen, Alfredo Cuzzocrea, Xiaoyong Du, Orhun Kara, Ting Liu,
Krishna M. Sivalingam, Dominik Ślęzak, Takashi Washio, and Xiaokang Yang

Editorial Board Members

More information about this series at http://www.springer.com/series/7899

Nitin Agarwal · Leonidas Sakalauskas ·
Gerhard-Wilhelm Weber (Eds.)

Modeling and Simulation of Social-Behavioral Phenomena in Creative Societies

First International EURO Mini Conference, MSBC 2019
Vilnius, Lithuania, September 18–20, 2019
Proceedings

Springer

Editors
Nitin Agarwal
Information Science Department
University of Arkansas at Little Rock
Little Rock, AR, USA

Leonidas Sakalauskas
Vilnius University
Vilnius, Lithuania

Gerhard-Wilhelm Weber
Faculty of Engineering Management
Poznan University of Technology
Poznan, Poland

ISSN 1865-0929   ISSN 1865-0937 (electronic)
Communications in Computer and Information Science
ISBN 978-3-030-29861-6   ISBN 978-3-030-29862-3 (eBook)
https://doi.org/10.1007/978-3-030-29862-3

This Springer imprint is published by the registered company Springer Nature Switzerland AG
The registered company address is: Gewerbestrasse 11, 6330 Cham, Switzerland

Preface

The growing challenges of societal sustainability, social complexity, behavioral operational research, and cohesion are becoming increasingly acknowledged worldwide. However, there is a conceptual and analytical gap in understanding the driving forces behind them. Thorough multidisciplinary research efforts are needed in order to make important contributions, starting from concepts and models, and ending with recommendations and decisions supporting systems capable of contributing to effective global and Europe-wide cultural and social policy formation agendas.

The application of computational models to study issues in the social sciences has been undergoing a rapid development during the last few decades. The conference Modeling and Simulation of Social-Behavioral Phenomena in Creative Societies (MSBC 2019) aims to create an open panel for an effective dialogue among researchers and practitioners, interested in the integration between computer science and social science, for strengthening the visibility and recognition, understanding the problems of simulation and modeling in social sciences, and providing developmental opportunities for young European scientists as well as students.

Since the challenges such as migration, globalization, radicalization of society, uneven economic growth and welfare distribution, social cohesion, etc., are closely connected with different levels of culture impact, the conference is focused, in particular, on modeling and simulation of concepts and models of modern culture and their impact on social capital and sustainability.

The papers in these proceedings cover the main topics and streams of the conference: social policy modeling and decision support systems; social cohesion modeling and metrics; concepts and models of the social capital; cultural behavioral modeling; concepts and models of creative societies and economies; globalization, society polarization, and cultural identity issues; operational research methodologies for societal complexity of cultural processes; behavioral operations research; affective computing and affective technologies; operational research (OR) and ethics: understanding dynamics of cultural processes; culture and sustainability: theoretical and methodological approach; agent-based social simulation systems; multi-agent systems and agent societies; and computational intelligence applications in social sciences.

This volume contains selected papers of the International Euro Mini Conference Modeling and Simulation of Social-Behavioral Phenomena in Creative Societies (MSBC 2019). The Program Committee selected the best of the papers submitted and an international board of reviewers reviewed all of them. In total, 26 submissions were received, 10 of which were accepted. The review process was single-blind and consisted of two rounds. On average, each paper was assigned to three reviewers and each reviewer was assigned two papers.

We cordially thank all the contributors for a successful conference.

Nitin Agarwal
Leonidas Sakalauskas
Gerhard-Wilhelm Weber

Organization

Program Chairs

Dorien Detombe   University of Amsterdam, The Netherlands
Rimvydas Lauzikas   Vilnius University, Lithuania

Organizing Chair

Leonidas Sakalauskas   Vilnius University, Lithuania

International Program Committee

Elena Andreeva	Hannover Medical School, Germany
Hamidreza Alipour	Shiraz Islamic Azad University, Iran
Abbas Aminifard	Shiraz Islamic Azad University, Iran
Akaki Arsenashvili	Tbilisi State University, Georgia
Valerie Belton	University of Strathclyde, UK
Nicolae Bulz	Economic and Social Cybernetic Commission, Romania
Cathal MacSwiney Brugha	College of Business, Ireland
Gordon Dash	University of Rhode Island, USA
Diana Cibulskiene	Siauliai University, Lithuania
Vitalijus Denisovas	Klaipeda University, Lithuania
Dorien DeTombe	Delft University of Technology, The Netherlands
Salvatore Greco	University of Catania, Italy
Ivan Izonin	Lviv Polytechnic National University, Ukraine
Januscz Holyst	Warsaw University of Technology, Poland
Ruta Kackute	Vilnius University, Lithuania
Nina Kajiji	University of Rhode Island, USA
George Klener	Central Economic Mathematical Institute, Russia
Jevgenij Kurilov	Vilnius Gediminas Technical University, Lithuania
Lyudmila Kuzmina	Kazan University, Russia
Rimvydas Lauzikas	Vilnius University, Lithuania
Ulrike Leopold-Wildburger	Karl-Franzens University, Austria
Herman Mawengkang	University of Sumatera Utara, Indonesia
Antoinette J. Muntjewerff	University of Amsterdam, The Netherlands
Amin Padash	Tarbiat Modaress University, Iran
Igor Nedelkovski	University of St. Kliment Ohridski, Macedonia
Don Petkov	Eastern Connecticut State University, USA
Darius Plikynas	Vilnius University, Lithuania
Leonidas Sakalauskas	Vilnius University, Lithuania
Luis Fernandez-Sanz	University of Alcala, Spain

External Reviewers

Gerhard-Wilhelm Weber   Poznan University of Technology, Poland
Adilson Elias Xavier   Federal University of Rio de Janeiro, Brazil
Edmundas Zavadskas   Vilnius Gediminas Technical University, Lithuania

Organizers

- European Association of Operational Research Societies (EURO)
- Vilnius University, Lithuania
- Vilnius Gediminas Technical University, Lithuania
- Ghent University, Belgium
- Lithuanian Operational Research Society (LitORS)

In Cooperation with

- Euro Working Group of OR and Development
- Euro Working Group on Experimental Economics
- EURO Working Group on Ethics and OR
- Lithuanian Culture Research Institute
- Lviv Polytechnic National University, Ukraine
- Warsaw University of Technology, Poland
- Klaipeda University, Lithuania
- Siauliai University, Lithuania

Supporters

- Lithuanian Research Council

Lithuanian OR Society

Contents

Computational Intelligence in Social Sciences

Social Disintegration Index and Its Applications   3
    Stanislovas Juknevicius

Optimization of Data Processing and Presentation in Social Surveys:
From Likert-Means to "Yes Percentage"   12
    Gediminas Merkys and Daiva Bubeliene

Modeling and Analysis of Social-Behavioral Processes

Modeling and Simulation of Impact and Control in Social Networks   29
    M. T. Agieva, A. V. Korolev, and G. A. Ougolnitsky

Finding Fake News Key Spreaders in Complex Social Networks by Using
Bi-Level Decomposition Optimization Method   41
    Mustafa Alassad, Muhammad Nihal Hussain, and Nitin Agarwal

An International Comparative Analysis for Autonomous Vehicles
and Their Effects   55
    Ryosuke Ando, Wei Liu, Jia Yang, and Yasuhide Nishihori

An Investigation of Social-Behavioral Phenomena in the Peer-Review
Processes of Scientific Foundations   68
    George Kleiner, Maxim Rybachuk, and Dmitry Ushakov

Agent-Based-Model of Students' Sociocognitive Learning Process
in Acquiring Tiered Knowledge   82
    Ismo T. Koponen

Modeling the Behaviour of Economic Agents as a Response to Information
on Tax Audits   96
    *Suriya Kumacheva, Elena Gubar, Ekaterina Zhitkova,
    and Galina Tomilina*

Behaviour Patterns in Expert Recognition by Means of Structured Expert
Judgement in Price Estimation in Customized Furniture Manufacturing   112
    *Birutė Mikulskienė, Viktor Medvedev, Tomas Vedlūga,
    and Olga Navickienė*

Towards Conceptually Novel Oscillating Agent-Based Simulation
of the Relationship Between Cultural Participation and Social Capital   126
  Rimvydas Laužikas and Darius Plikynas

Author Index   145

Computational Intelligence in Social Sciences

Social Disintegration Index
and Its Applications

Stanislovas Juknevicius[(✉)]

Lithuanian Culture Research Institute, Saltoniskiu 58, 08105 Vilnius, Lithuania
juknevicius.s@gmail.com

Abstract. This article presents the calculation methodology of the social disintegration index (SDIx) and an analysis of its applications. Social disintegration is interpreted as a lack of integration, and the Social Disintegration Index is calculated as a value supplementing the average of various social integration indicators to the figure of one. This index allows comparison of groups and societies according to the elasticity of relations between their members and can be compared to Social Network Index (SNI) or Social, Cultural and Civic Integration Index (SCCII). Another application of SDIx is in suicide analysis. In this case, Social Disintegration Index may be used to validate Emile Durkheim's theory of suicides. And, finally, the SDIx may be applied to the construction of certain models of human behavior. In this case, we presume that social disintegration means behavioral changes which, in their turn, are determined by the changes in stimuli (typical situations) and mentalities.

Keywords: Social Disintegration Index · Social integration · Behavior · Suicides · Stimulus-reaction model · Mentalities

1 Introduction

The processes of social disintegration can be studied by using two main approaches. Firstly, processes which destroy social cohesion can be identified, sorted and analyzed. According to Robert Fedderke and Johannes Kushner, social disintegration refers to such dimensions as conflict and instability, breakdowns in political and civil rights, crime and violence, growing divisions between rich and poor, and eroding levels of citizens' satisfaction with their lives [1]. On the other hand, social disintegration can be regarded as a lack of integration, and so the focus can be on the analysis of indicators which reflect social integration. This paper adopts the latter approach.

Social networks play an important role in both social integration and disintegration processes [2]. The Berkman–Syme Social Network Index (SNI) [3, 4] assesses participation in 12 types of social relationships. These include relations with spouse, children, parents, parents-in-law, other close family members, close neighbors, friends, workmates, schoolmates, fellow volunteers, members of groups without religious affiliation, and religious groups. One point is assigned for each type of relationship for which respondents indicate that they speak (in person or on the phone) to person in that relationship at least once every two weeks. Social Network Index allows researchers to categorize individuals into four levels of social connection: socially

© Springer Nature Switzerland AG 2019
N. Agarwal et al. (Eds.): MSBC 2019, CCIS 1079, pp. 3–11, 2019.
https://doi.org/10.1007/978-3-030-29862-3_1

isolated (individuals with low intimate contacts—not married, fewer than six friends or relatives, and no membership in community groups); moderately isolated; moderately integrated; and socially integrated. SNI is mainly used to study the impact of social connectedness on health [5, 6].

Wong and Tezli [7] considered nineteen variables for the creation of an index to measure the social, cultural, and civic integration of immigrants. These variables included volunteering, voting in elections, sense and extensiveness of trust in people, experience of discrimination, and others. Eight variables remained using the statistical technique of factor analysis, and these eight constituted Social, Cultural and Civic Integration Index (SCCII).

The methodology presented in the paper differs from the other ones in that it includes a formula which allows to range the countries by level of social disintegration. The Idea of SDIx has emerged in the process of investigation of the role of social disintegration for suicides. Emile Durkheim is credited to be the first to demonstrate that the suicide rate provided a measure of social disintegration [8, 9]. On the other hand, some researchers argue that a close study of Durkheim's evidence supports the opposite conclusion and that the incidence of self-destructive behaviors such as suicide is often greatest among those with high levels of social integration [10]. Which of the opinions can be empirically confirmed or denied? To put it in other words, does correlation between suicides and social disintegration exist? We couldn't apply any of the existing social integration indexes to solve the problem, so created a new one. Other SDIx applications were considered later too. Both the SDIx formula (1) and the formula for typical behavior studies (2) are introduced for the first time; therefore, they can be improved. On the other hand, in its current form, the formula (1) can already be applied successfully to range the countries and to study relationship between social disintegration and suicides.

2 Social Disintegration Index

The focus of this section of the article is the analysis of the behavior, as it is the changes in behavior that best reflect social integration or disintegration. The main form of behavior reflecting social integration is participation in common activities. The range of such activities can be rather extensive, starting with a friendly chat over a cup of coffee and ending with an armed battle behind the barricades. The study of different aspects of these activities requires application of different indicators. Two types of social integration indicators can be distinguished: simple and complex. The simple indicator allows examination of one particular aspect of social integration, for example: participation in city festivals, communication with neighbors, etc. In social surveys, this aspect of social integration is studied with the help of dichotomous questions (yes/no). Meanwhile, complex indicators comprise two or more simple indicators. In social surveys, this aspect of social integration is studied with the help of such questions as "which of the activities listed below do you participate in".

Let's say that the society comprises N members, N' part of which participates in the common activity n. In this case, the social integration indicator can be calculated as a ratio of the indicator n and N' of people participating in common activities. For example, if a third of residents of a certain city participate in city festivals, a quarter participate in political actions, while one in six residents regularly goes to sports clubs, the social integration indicator calculated with the help of these three indicators will be equal to 0.25 (1/3 + 1/4 + 1/6 divided by 3). The value supplementing this indicator to 1 shall be called the Social Disintegration Index, which is calculated according to this formula:

$$SDIx = 1 - \frac{\sum_{i=1}^{n} N_i'}{n} \tag{1}$$

As shown by the formula, the Social Disintegration Index varies within the range [0; 1]. It is equal to a 0, where all members of the society analyzed participate in the activities reflecting social integration, and it is equal to 1 where nobody participates in these activities.

We will now calculate the social disintegration index in different European countries on the basis of the 1999–2000 data of the European Values Study [11]. The survey was chosen because some of its results have been published by Halman [12] and can be compared with the results of two previous (1990 and 1981) and two subsequent (2008 and 2017) studies. Social integration will be measured using 25 simple indicators combined with 3 complex indicators.

One of the main indicators reflecting social integration is the number of people doing unpaid voluntary work. In the EVS questionnaire, this aspect of social integration is studied with the help of question 5(b): *Which, if any, are you currently doing unpaid voluntary work for? Social welfare services for elderly, handicapped or deprived people; religious or church organizations; education, arts, music or cultural activities; trade unions; political parties or groups; local community action on issues like poverty, employment, housing, racial equality; third world development or human rights; conservation, the environment, ecology, animal rights; professional associations; youth work (e.g. scouts, guides, youth clubs etc.); sports or recreation; women's groups; peace movements; voluntary organizations concerned with health; other groups.*

Another form of social integration is participation or readiness to participate in political actions. In the EVS questionnaire, this aspect of integration is reflected in question 51: *Now I would like you to look at this card. I'm going to read out some different forms of political action that people can take, and I'd like you to tell me for each one, weather you have actually done any of these things, whether you might do it or would never, under any circumstances, do it.*

A Singing a petition; B Joining in boycotts; C Attending lawful demonstrations; D Joining unofficial strikes; E Occupying buildings or factories.

Social integration can also be measured by how often people spend time together. In the EVS questionnaire, this aspect of social integration is studied with the help of question 6: *I'm going to ask how often you do certain things? Spend time with friends; Spend time with colleagues; Spend time in church, mosque or synagogue; Spend time in clubs and voluntary associations;*

The survey results are presented in Table 1: Column *N'1* provides the share of respondents whose answer to question 5(b) was 'Yes' to at least one of the listed voluntary activities. Column $N'2$ provides share of respondents whose answers to the question 51 was "Have actually done". Column $N'3$ provides the share of respondents whose answer to at least one of the activities listed in question 6 was "Every week". Column SDIx provides the countries' disintegration indexes calculated according to formula (1); column Suic. R provides the suicide mortality rate (per 100 000 population) in those countries in the same year. Several countries have not been including into the table, the data on which has not been found at the World Health Organization Database [13].

Table 1. Social disintegration indexes, social integration indicators and suicide rates in 28 European countries in year 2000. Sources: European Values Study Database; Loek Halman. The European Values Study: A Third Wave. World Health Organization Database.

Country	$N'1$	$N'2$	$N'3$	SDIx	Suic.R
Russia	0.07	0.08	0.16	0.90	39
Lithuania	0.12	0.09	0.15	0.88	44
Hungary	0.14	0.05	0.18	0.88	32
Ukraine	0.12	0.08	0.20	0.87	30
Romania	0.14	0.06	0.20	0.87	13
Poland	0.12	0.07	0.23	0.86	15
Estonia	0.16	0.07	0.21	0.85	27
Bulgaria	0.15	0.07	0.27	0.84	17
Latvia	0.18	0.10	0.23	0.83	32
Belarus	0.18	0.06	0.29	0.82	35
Slovenia	0.25	0.11	0.28	0.79	30
Germany	0.19	0.18	0.25	0.79	13
Portugal	0.12	0.15	0.36	0.79	5
Croatia	0.23	0.11	0.38	0.76	20
Austria	0.28	0.17	0.26	0.76	20
Czech Republic	0.30	0.20	0.21	0.76	16
France	0.23	0.29	0.24	0.75	17
Iceland	0.32	0.19	0.25	0.75	11
Italy	0.25	0.23	0.28	0.75	7
Malta	0.28	0.13	0.34	0.75	6
Greece	0.31	0.20	0.27	0.74	3
Finland	0.37	0.16	0.28	0.73	23
Belgium	0.32	0.28	0.26	0.71	21
Ireland	0.28	0.20	0.40	0.71	12
Denmark	0.33	0.27	0.29	0.70	14
Netherlands	0.31	0.26	0.34	0.70	9
Great Britain	0.43	0.24	0.33	0.67	7
Sweden	0.54	0.33	0.31	0.61	13

The table shows that the highest social disintegration indexes are reported in Eastern Europe, with the lowest indexes in Northern and West Europe. These regions largely differ in both social capital and development of civil society too [14]. The next step of the survey is the study of the SDIx dynamics and its relation to other indexes applied to compare society's and, in the basis of results obtained through comparison, seek for the most efficient methods for enhancement of social integration.

The formula (1) can be improved in two basic ways. Firstly, the range of social integration indicators can be expanded. Obviously, the higher the number of social integration indicators included into the analysis, the more accurate the social disintegration index is. On the other hand, the higher the number of indicators distinguished, the more doubts can arise with respect to the significance of a certain indicator. Secondly, the formula (1) interprets all indicators as being equivalent, which is definitely not always the case. For example, one can assume that the social integration of people fighting side by side behind the barricades is stronger than that of people who discuss political news over a cup of coffee. In this case, the introduction of coefficients of social integration indicators is necessary, however, this problem requires a separate study.

3 Suicides as Disintegration

The scholarly literature marks out social, economic, psychological, physiological reasons for a suicide [15, 16]. To our opinion, the concept of disintegration is crucial for understanding causes of suicides. We chose two kinds of disintegration to analyze in this paper: disintegration of the nations and disintegration of the individuals. The first kind of disintegration means the loss of national identity and/or political independence by the nations resulting from military intervention or from adverse historical circumstances, the second means social disintegration.

Disintegration of the nations was mainly responsible for the dynamics of suicides in the West in the twentieth century – that is the threat for the existence of some nations resulting from adverse historical circumstances. Austrians, Estonians, Hungarians and Czechoslovakians were leading the suicide rates before the Second World War. All these nations had serious problems with political independence and national identity. When Austro-Hungarian monarchy, one of the most powerful monarchies in Europe, fell – Austria became a small state, having to deal, apart from everything else, with all the economic, social and moral consequences of losing the war. However, this state soon found its own place in new Europe and was no longer on the list of the leaders in suicides. Hungarians got their independence in 1919, after a struggle of more than three centuries for their unified sovereign state, just to lose it again in 1945. Estonia's fight for an independent state was also full of dramatics. Czechoslovakia – a political neologism born in 1919, was not able to perceive either its identity, or its historical prospects in time. Unsteadiness of this creation was proved by the split in 1993.

Lithuania, Russia, Byelorussia and Latvia were leading in suicides at the end of the twentieth century. Unexpected to some, Lithuania's leadership in this context is more than comprehensible: during the last two centuries (according to some authors, ever since the times of Vytautas the Great) Lithuania has enjoyed its independence for approximately 30 years only. Latvia's way to independence was no easier. Byelorussia did not even dream of creating their independent state. Russians experienced and are still experiencing all the consequences of the falling empire.

There is a feature common to the dynamics of suicides among the nations that have fought for their independence which may be named as an overdue effect: most people commit suicides not during their struggle for independence, but after the declaration of independence. This fact is common almost among all nations that have gained their independence in the twentieth century: Hungary, Finland, Baltic States and Iceland. This phenomenon might be explained by at least two groups of reasons. On one hand, the fight for independence is an important factor unifying the nation, however dramatic and full of losses it might be. When the struggle is over this factor disappears and the nation experiences a certain existential vacuum. Old goals are reached, and the new ones are not formed yet. Respectively, the risk of suicides increases, and its number grows.

Let's come back to the role of social disintegration for suicides. Our study has revealed that suicide is linked with social disintegration. Pearson correlation coefficients between $N'1$, $N'2$, $N'3$ and the suicide rates are equal to correspondingly -0.921, -0.901 and -0.581 (all correlations are significant at the 0.01 level). The correlation coefficient between SDIx and suicide rates is equal to 0.611 (correlations is significant at the 0.01 level). This means that social disintegration does play an important role in the causes of suicide. This *inter alia* means that the more people communicate, the less inclined they are to suicide.

4 Mentalities and Behavior

The S-R (stimulus-response) model which is widely applied in behavioral sciences, enables explanation of some behavioral variants, but does have deficiencies as well. First of all, response is given only in such cases where there is a stimulus, i.e. the formula expressing this model should be as follows: *if there is S, then there is R*. Moreover, different people respond differently to the same stimuli and some people do not respond to them at all. In this study, we will presume that different responses are determined by different features of mentalities (M). For instance, only those people in whose life feature of mentality such as *godliness* plays a bigger or smaller role, make the sign of the cross when walking past the altar of a church. If we mark the altar as S1, godliness as M1 and the sign of the cross as R1, we can express the dependency existing between these variables as follows: *if there are S1 and M1, then there is R1*. The formula of this behavioral model would be as follows.

$$If\ Sn\ and\ Mn,\ then\ Rn \qquad (2)$$

Let's consider each part of this formula in more detail. Objects or phenomena perceived through the five senses often trigger responses. For example, when a person meets his/her acquaintance on the street, he/she says 'hello', and when a person sees an animal which poses a threat to his/her life, he/she runs or takes evasive action, etc. However, in the majority of cases the reason behind every human behavior lies in the world of imagination rather than in the world perceived through the five senses;

therefore, if we want to explain this group of stimuli, we need to analyze imagination contents, the main ones of which are archetypes and symbols [17]. Both of these manifest themselves in *typical situations*. If the concept of a stimuli is likely to define the biological aspect of human behavior, then typical situations describe the social aspect of that human behavior.

The most frequently mentioned traits or mentalities include duty, consciousness, empathy, love of one's homeland, hatred towards people of a different race (religion), etc. As the features of mentality are expressed in concepts, we should create a thesaurus of different features of mentality characteristic of the analyzed society. The mentalities of specific groups or individuals comprising the society would be part of this thesaurus.

Responses constitute the only one element of human behavior which is available for empirical observation and measurement. Typical behavior plays an exceptional role among different types of responses. There are two main sources of typical behavior of members of a society: statistical data and results of social surveys. Statistics includes data on various aspects of the social, economic, cultural and political life (participation in cultural events and political campaigns, consumption of goods and services, etc.). Findings of social surveys supplement these data with information about the attitudes, values, beliefs, behavior of members of a society.

Society is a system where people are distinguished for certain features of mentalities, behave in certain typical ways in certain typical situations. All the elements of this system are interlinked: changes in typical situations lead to mentality and behavioral changes, mentality changes alter typical situations and behavior. Typical behavior constantly changes. The main objective of research is to explain these changes. What kinds of changes in the area of typical situations and mentalities lead to changes in typical behavior?

Suicide is a variant of typical behavior. The findings of our studies confirmed that social disintegration has an impact on suicides. Therefore, what mentality traits encourage or, on the contrary, suppress social disintegration? Moreover, how are these traits related to suicides? The EVS surveys give at least a partial answer to these questions.

Question 80 of the EVS is aimed to find out which part of the population is ready to do something to improve the conditions of various social groups in their countries, and questions 81 is intended to find out the reasons to do something to help the elderly people and is formulated as follows: *There can be several reasons to do something to help the elderly people in your country. Please tell me for each reason I am going to read out, if they apply to you or not. A Because you feel you have a moral duty to help; B Because you sympathize with them; C Because it is in the interest of society; D Because it is in your own interest; E To do something in return.*

These reasons to do something to help the elderly people are features of mentalities which take the form of typical behavior in typical situations. One of these features, namely a moral duty is related to suicide: the correlation coefficient between the Suic. R. and a part of the population, whose main reasons to do something to help the elderly people is a duty, is equal to -0.616 (correlation is significant at the 0.01 level). Actually, this confirms Kant's views that suicides are the loss of duty to self and to society [18].

5   Discussion

The three SDIx applications distinguished in the paper can be treated as three phases of the same process. Firstly, the SDIx enables the ranking of various countries according to the level of social disintegration. Depending on the indicators used in the formula (1), the same country's position in the ranking may change, but, regardless, the ranking allows both similarities and differences existing among various countries to be analyzed. In the next phase of research, we will be able to look for a relationship between the Social Disintegration Index and other indexes that reflect social processes, such as the Global Index of Religion and Atheism, the Corruption Index, etc. The paper highlights the relationship between the SDIx and suicide rates. The third phase analyses the reasons for changes in social indicators. The paper discusses two groups of drivers behind these changes – typical situations and mentality features and reveals the relationship between duty and suicide.

The final purpose of typical behavior research is to develop a model which is able to explain changes in typical behavior. The process of developing such a model primarily depends on theoretical approaches which are the basis for different models. Let's consider two of them.

Pitirim Sorokin classified societies according to their cultural mentality, which can be "ideational", "sensate" or "idealistic" (a synthesis of the two). According ti him, major civilizations evolve from an ideational to an idealistic, and eventually to a sensate mentality. He suggested that in the twentieth century the sensate Western society began to fall apart. There was, among other things, a disintegration of its legal, moral, esthetic values which, from within, control and guide the behavior of individuals and groups [19]. Some aspects of this process can be measured with the help of SDIx.

von Bertalnfy argued against robotatization of man, toward a humanization of science in his book *Organismic Psychology and Systems Theory* [20]. The main purpose of the author was to outline the place of psychology in modern science and briefly to review a new Natural Philosophy which appears to be emerging. According to Bertalanfy, in order to understand the processes which take place in society, that society should be viewed as a system in which symbols play an important role. In this case, formula (1) can be used to explore symbols as stimuli for common activities.

6   Conclusion

In its current form, the Social Disintegration Index can be applied successfully to rank the states by level of social disintegration, as well as for analyzing the relationships between social disintegration and suicides. In order to apply this index to create or investigate human behavior models, it will be necessary to adopt additional assumptions and define the concepts used in developing such a model.

References

1. Klitgaard, R., Fedderke, J.: Social integration and disintegration: an exploratory analysis of cross-country data. World Dev. **23**(3), 357–369 (1995)
2. Kadushin, C.: Understanding Social Networks: Theories, Concepts, and Findings. Oxford University Press, New York (2012)
3. Berkman, L.F., Syme, S.L.: Social networks, host resistance, and mortality: a nine-year follow-up of Alameda county residents. Am. J. Epidemiol. **109**, 186–204 (1979)
4. Berkman, L.F., Breslow, L.: Health and Ways of Living: the Alameda County Study. Oxford University Press, New York (1983)
5. Lubben, J.: Assessing social networks among elderly populations. Family Commun. Health: J. Health Promot. Maintenance **11**, 42–52 (1988)
6. Berkman, L.F., Glass, T.: Social integration, social networks, social support and health. In: Berkman, L.F., Kawachi, I. (eds.) Social Epidemiology, pp. 158–162. Oxford University Press, New York (2000)
7. Wong, L.L., Tezli, A.: Mesuring social, cultural and civic integration in Canada: the creation of an index and some applications. Can. Ethn. Stud. **45**(3), 9–37 (2013)
8. Berrios, G.E., Mohanna, M.: Durkheim and French psychiatric views on suicide during the 19th century: a conceptual history. Br. J. Psychiatry **156**(1), 1–9 (1990)
9. Hassana, R.: One hundred years of Emile Durkheim's suicide: a study in sociology. Aust. N. Z. J. Psychiatry **32**(2), 168–171 (1998)
10. Kushner, H.I., Sterk, C.E.: The limits of social capital: Durkheim, suicide, and social cohesion. Am. J. Public Health **95**(7), 1139–1143 (2005)
11. European Values Study Database. https://europeanvaluesstudy.eu/methodology-data-documentation
12. Halman, L.: The European Values Study: A Third Wave. Source Book of the 1999/2000 European Values Study Surveys. Tilburg University Press, Tilburg (2001)
13. World Health Organisation Database. https://www.who.int/gho/mental_health/suicide_rates/en/
14. Arts, W., Hagenaars, J., Halman, L. (eds.): The Cultural Diversity of European Unity: Findings, Explanations and Reflections from the European Values Study. Brill, Leiden (2003)
15. Bering, J.: Suicidal: Why We Kill Ourselves. University of Chicago Press, Chicago (2018)
16. Dos Santos, J.P., Tavers, M., Barros, P.P.: More than just numbers: suicide rates and economic cycle in Portugal (1910–2013). SSM – Popul. Health **2**, 14–23 (2016)
17. Juknevicius, S.: Imagining communities and imagined worlds: the archetypal concept of history. Sovijus. Interdisc. Stud. Cult. **3**(1), 67–79 (2015)
18. Kant, I.: Grundlegung zur Metaphysik der Sitten. Hrsg., eingel. und erl. von Jens Timmermann. Vandenhoeck & Ruprecht, Göttingen (2004). Die Erstausgabe 1785
19. Sorokin, P.A.: The Basic Trends of our Time. Rowman & Littlefield, Lanham (1964)
20. von Bertalanfy, L.: Organismic Psychology and Systems Theory. Clark University Press, Worcwster (1968)

Optimization of Data Processing and Presentation in Social Surveys: From Likert-Means to "Yes Percentage"

Gediminas Merkys[1]([✉]) and Daiva Bubeliene[2]

[1] Vytautas Magnus University, 44248 Kaunas, Lithuania
kadagysgm@gmail.com
[2] Kaunas University of Applied Sciences,
Pramones pr. 20, 50468 Kaunas, Lithuania
daivabubeliene@gmail.com

Abstract. The article presents a replication study of a significant empirical study carried out earlier. Borg, Gabler (2002) showed that there is an extremely high correlation between the Means of Likert Scale Items and the percentage of agreement (Yes%). On this basis, they suggested to use not traditional Likert mean, but Yes % in survey reports. The latter are easier to interpret and do not have the same problem as Equidistance of Likert-type scales. It was decided, based on the big date (N ≈ 9000), to carry out the replication study in another historical time, in another culture and measuring another construct. If the statistical regularity detected by Borg, Gabler is repeated, it is universal, then it is really appropriate to move to a wider use of Yes% when preparing the survey report. The replication study showed that there is an extremely high correlation ($R^2 = 0.948$) between the primary Likert items means and Yes% of items, approximating to the linear function. Used the classic 5-grade Likert scale. The verification is carried out only at the level of single items without passing to the level of analysis of additive indexes. It also turned out that the Likert items-mean correlation with the No% is lower ($R^2 = 0.865$), which negates the postulate of symmetry of the scale. In addition, the Likert means correlation with "neutral category%" is even lower - $R^2 = 0.340$. When preparing Survey studies reports, give priority to "yes %" instead of Likert items means.

Keywords: Likert scale · Equidistance · Agreement percentage · Correlation · Reports of social survey

1 Introduction: Theoretical and Practical Context of the Study

Social sciences have been using mathematical methods for a long time. The use of measurement, experiment and mathematical modelling is one of the reasons why the social sciences have diverged from the humanities and became independent fields of study. Social surveys are one such area where mathematical-statistical methods are applied. However, the methodology employed in the creation and the use of surveys is still characterised by the lack of development of any original mathematical models of

© Springer Nature Switzerland AG 2019
N. Agarwal et al. (Eds.): MSBC 2019, CCIS 1079, pp. 12–25, 2019.
https://doi.org/10.1007/978-3-030-29862-3_2

the social phenomenon. Data are simply analyzed by well-known and accepted statistical tools such as normal distribution or chi-squared and nonparametrical functions, linear regression, factor and cluster analysis, latent class analysis, Rasch-model etc. Recently more mathematically-inclined social scientists have started to employ the elegant mathematical apparatus in their questionnaires and tests which allows them to comprehensively model the behaviour of the survey response. Such attempts fall under the term Item Response Theory (IRT), [8, 11, 25].

Evidently, mathematical-statistical methods must be applied correctly such that the conditions of the model used are satisfied. Contrary to soft sciences, where many observations can be explained away by pluralism and a multitude of paradigms, the use of mathematics and statistics remains strictly in the domain of hard sciences. If a mistake is made in the model, then the output will increase it tenfold simultaneously masking it under the authority of mathematics. Thus, the moral is simple: either mathematical-statistical methods are not to be used at all or they ought to be used correctly. The point is driven further by the fact that fully legitimate qualitative methods are spreading massively in the practice of social research [2, 19].

This paper wishes to attract attention to one specific problem of applied statistics: the use of some classical statistical parameters of interest, widely used and accepted in social surveys, is of questionable correctness. We hope that such doubt will encourage a discussion and possibly even the revision of established practices and views. In particular, we address the massively-used Likert scale, named after the American psychologist Likert (1903–1981) [20]. The aforementioned scale is universal and easy to use. These are probably the reasons for the non-decaying popularity and application of the scale to this day.

The respondents are given a set of sensible statements (psychometric stimuli) and are asked to register their answers in a uniform format next to each statement. The uniform format encompasses several gradations of the answers: from complete agreement to complete disagreement. The most common categories are: "I strongly disagree", "I disagree", "I have no opinion", "I agree", "I strongly agree". The classical version of the scale has five levels of gradation where two correspond to agreement, two to disagreement and the middle category corresponds to a neutral answer "no opinion". The answers are then quantified by agreement into scores from 1 to 5 or from 0 to 4.

Over time many more modifications of the scale were introduced. Such as scales that have the middle neutral category removed and scores encoded from 1 to 4 or from 1 to 6 points, or the version with 7 categories including the neutral one [7, 14, 15, 21]. Nevertheless, despite the number of categories, the distinguishing attributes of the Likert scale are its bipolarity and symmetry. The respondents are given an equal number of positive and negative (of agreement and disagreement) gradations.

Practice shows that researchers sometimes work with estimates derived from single statements. However, usually an additive index is computed from the answers of multiple statements that are unified by a common theme. Either the sum or the mean of the scores is found. In this case we speak of psychometric approach. It is postulated that the given diagnostic statements are of equal weight chosen randomly from the set of all statements. The estimates of additive indices comprise a manifest variable which is then used to indirectly infer the latent variable - the consciousness-construct of the individual or group in question [13, 26].

In an ideal case the calculated additive index must correctly differentiate the subjects by the latent construct. The creation of the additive index is controlled by psychometric statistics tools, reliability control, factor validation and, currently, Item Response Theory. Yet even in respectable research a statement or an estimate derived from it is taken for granted. Notwithstanding, the validity of a psychometric test begins with the validity of a single item.

Statements in Likert scale can be formulated about a subject's inner mental state or behaviour patterns, in which case we speak of self-evaluation. That is the case in all clinical or self-concept questionnaires, research on happiness, personnel questionnaires (on work motivation, job satisfaction) and so on. Further, statements can be on: (a) concrete objective outside objects - a brand logo, holiday destination, political entity etc. (b) on views and attitudes on universal values etc. Nowadays we could hardly find a thematic direction in social research and social surveys where the Likert scale is not used. It is used in clinical, work and organizational psychology, pedagogical psychology, socialization research, educational research, surveys on values, healthy lifestyle, politics and consumer behaviour etc. Unsurprisingly, many papers are published on the usage of Likert scale, a methodological discourse is ongoing [5, 12, 16, 18].

A correct use of a Likert scale requires that a few formal conditions be satisfied which, unfortunately, are not always guaranteed in practice: the statistical independence of statements (items). If we permute the statements, that is, change the order in which the statements are given in a survey, it should, ideally, not have any impact on the respondent's measured opinion or view in the result. This problem can easily be solved for online surveys. Every time a survey window is opened, a random number generator produces a random order of the statements for each subject. Then the data fall into a matrix by a predefined order. Lamentably, many social survey platforms do not have this function, even though they should [1].

However, there is one problem of the Likert scale that has not been solved to this day. It may happen that it never will be completely. It is obvious that the 5 or 7 grade scale is a typical ordinal scale. In this case equal distances between the grades of the scale, which is something that social scientists have been dreaming about for a long time and what an interval scale formally requires, cannot be guaranteed in any way. There is no such equal grading in a Likert scale, it is simply postulated. Thus, the estimates of a Likert scale do not differ in any way from, say, a quasi-scale of school grades which was not taken seriously even at the turn of 19th - 20th centuries. Hence there is a real problem that is usually ignored. It is not entirely correct to compute the mean and the variance - the parameters of a normal distribution - from an ordinal scale. Unfortunately, by cloaking behind the equal grading postulate and the established practice ("it has always been done this way"), the social survey reports, papers and dissertations give the means and standard deviations of the data in a Likert scale. This is done with single-item estimates as well as the estimates of additive indices.

The aforementioned problem of using ordinal data as if it were of an interval is not the only one. Quite honestly, this problem can even be relaxed. We can assume that the measured and existing latent constructs (characteristics of the human psyche), their expression, can in principle be properly measured quantitatively on an interval or even a ratio scale. It is just that currently the social and behavioural sciences do not yet have the necessary technological capabilities. The development of neurosciences shines expectantly in this context. Even now there are data, bold hypotheses, that the content of human social attitudes and their expression has a connection with deep brain processes [6, 17].

The latter, as is known, can already be observed by objective study methods of brain activity or neurochemical reactions. Maybe one day a reliable bridge between traditional surveys and the objective data of neuroscience will be established?

In principle, it might be possible to postulate that the Likert scale generally reflects the measured characteristics of a human mind, it just does it approximately, in a slightly distorted way. Some mathematical formalities are not held. In the spirit of the history of natural sciences we could say that Pascal's mercury thermometer is also an imprecise measurement device since some of the heat energy is consumed by the thermometer itself. If science could not measure something exactly, then it persistently and consistently tried to do it approximately. And there is no constructive alternative to this attitude of scientists. Analogously it is possible to tolerate the limitations of the Likert scale and it is no secret that the majority of researchers do. There is another argument in favour of the Likert scale. It is known from the central limit theorem in probability theory and statistics that if one has a large enough sample, then the sample mean converges in distribution to a normal distribution [9]. It is constantly encountered that in the statistical analysis of the survey data. If an additive index of a Likert scale is formed from at least 15–20 primary items and the number of studied subjects is $N > 500$, then the resulting distribution is close to a normal distribution.

Thus, in this context the authors of this paper have raised the problems of Likert scale's equal distances and normality, they have likewise vindicated its use. It is possible to discuss the impact that these problems have on the quality of data analysis of social surveys. The existence of the two aforementioned problems cannot be denied. Whatever the case, besides the two discussed Likert scale problems, there exists yet another problem of no less importance. It, apart from a few exceptions, is not even discussed. We shall look at this problem in more detail.

No measurement in the practice of life, nor in science, is an end in itself. The measurement procedure is always a part of some concrete meaningful theoretical context. It means that the result of a measurement is always interpreted. The most universal definition of a measurement is this: the assignment of numerical values to an object, phenomenon or a relation between them. The point is that the assigned numerical value must be interpreted. Ideally, the zero, the minimum and the maximum values of the scale ought to have an objective meaning. In the absence of such objectivity the zero of a scale can be chosen by convention.

Psychometric measurements are ontologically and epistemologically probably most closely related to biometric measurements. The latter have a big advantage since the norm of a given value is more or less known to everyone. Suppose we have the values of a person's weight, height, blood pressure, blood sugar level and various other parameters. Their essence is easily understood and can immediately be sensibly interpreted. The same can be said of measurements that are based on an accepted currency (in Euros, US Dollars). If we needed to interpret the measurement results based on Venezuelan Bolivar (Fuerte Bolivar), whose nominal value drastically changes every day, then we would immediately face difficulties interpreting. The result of a given measurement would not be so clear outright. The problem is that the estimates of a Likert scale, from the point of view of measurement interpretation, are more complicated than the Venezuelan Bolivar.

If a simple additive index is constructed, then its score depends on the number of statements involved and on the number of possible answers next to each statement. The more primary items and the more categories there are, the larger the maximum possible value of the additive index will be. The authors of this paper has once had to form an additive Likert scale index which was composed of 160 (!) primary items and five categories. Cases where an additive Likert index is comprised of 15–20 primary items are encountered tens of thousands of times in the practice of social surveys. In the prior case we speak of a widely used psychometric inventory "safe school - safe child" which addresses older students [4, 22].

From the logical and factor analysis of 160 primary items 38 subscales are formed. Secondary factor analysis shows that we can freely form a total score. This way the raw total score can range from 160 to 800. If computed an average should fit between 1 and 5 or 0 and 4 points, depending on the encoding. As is known, the raw score and an average are related by a linear transformation on a scale while the correlation coefficient between these two values is always one.

The bounds of the scale's range are not entirely clear. In the case of a Likert scale neither the researcher nor the client who commissioned the survey, nor the consumer is sure what the computed value of an estimate from a single individual or the mean of a group really means. Of course, it is possible to see whether the estimate of an individual or a group has crossed (or not crossed) the formal zero reference point of the scale. The problem will be reduced if the raw scores are transformed into the z-score of a standard normal distribution. We encourage social scientists to do this since then by inductive statistical explanation we could at least find a temporary zero of the scale that corresponds to the mean of the standardized sample. With each increment of the standardized sample this zero becomes more and more accurate. But this is a topic for another paper (on the necessity to apply statistical standardization more widely when presenting the results of surveys).

Whatever the case, a question arises: why do social scientists so often report the mean and the standard deviation from raw Likert scores? Such estimates, first of all, are not entirely correct from a purely formal mathematical perspective and, secondly, are hard to interpret in practice. Is this due to tradition? It is clear that this tradition is not entirely adequate if not to say malicious.

Some researchers have taken notice that the results of a Likert scale are best presented in the form of "agreement percentage" or "yes percentage" [3]. For clarity the so called "yes %" on a five-grade Likert scale is found by summing over the response frequency of the last two categories (corresponding to agreement). Borg, Gabler (2002) have done statistical reanalysis of four large surveys, each having a sample of tens of thousands. The surveys were on personnel and organizational psychology. The authors gave empirical proof that there exists a tight linear relationship ($r^2 \approx 0.98 \approx 0.99$) between Likert means and the yes percentages approximating a functional dependence. Such strong repeated systemic relationship practically means that Likert mean and "yes %" are essentially the same thing. Well, formally speaking, the values are not the same, however, it is obvious that what they measure or reflect is common to both. This conclusion opens an innovative overturn in the process of social survey result analysis and, especially, in their presentation to the professional or public audience. What is this optimistic interpretation based on? Contrary to the mean of a Likert scale, an estimator such as agreement percentage is impeccable from a formal mathematical perspective. The data arranged in a non-decreasing order is a manifest variable that has an objective origin. It shows which percentage of subjects reacted to a written stimulus (statement) with agreement. Yes % forms a dichotomic scale "yes/no". As is known, a dichotomic scale satisfies the conditions of a "higher-level" scale - an interval scale. Furthermore, if a sample is large enough, the relative data are approximately normally distributed, See: Moivre-Laplace Theorem and Central Limit Theorem, (Normal Approximation to the Binomial Distribution) [10].

Moreover, if 50% of respondents in a population X and 25% of respondents in a population Y agree with a statement-stimulus "A", then we are justified in performing the operation of division and saying that one population has twice the frequency of another population. We can let go of the notion of frequency and claim that the quantitative expression of a measured attribute in a population X is expressed twice as strongly than in population Y. In this instance a meaningfully applied operation of division would even let us talk of a ratio (absolute) scale. On the contrary, we could not say anything like that for a ranked scale. For example, if on a 10-point scale of high-school grades where 10 is the highest mark one student receives a score of 10 and another a score of 5, we cannot conclude that one knows twice as much as the other.

It is especially important that the agreement percentage is very simple, clear and easy to interpret for the researcher, the client who commissioned the survey and its results for the public consumer. It is characteristic of most social surveys that their results do not lie dormant in the archives of the researchers or the university, but falls into public discourse through mass media and forms the societies' self-concept and public opinion. It is an important attribute of a democratic society and a public good. Note that there are not social surveys in China, North Korea, Turkmenistan and other autocratic countries. We can say that the conversion of mathematically expressed survey results into layman's language is a public good.

Let us return to the inventory example "Safe school - safe child". It has a subscale on "Conflict&Aggression in the school yard" which is composed of 9 primary items. It is pointless to give the raw score of this subscale since it is uninterpretable. The averages of single Likert items are similarly senseless. There is a possibility to use "yes percentages" and to express the result of the measurement in a much more informative fashion. For instance, to 9 stimuli, indicating the lack of safety in the school yard, the respondents reacted with an average agreement reaching 13%. Individual scores of the 9 indicators of unsafe school yard environment varied between 7,9 and 19,1%.

Whatever the case, the doubtful practice of submitting Likert scale means in the reports of social research is not waning. On the other hand, attempts to use "yes %" in the report do not catch on.

The author's of the paper has accumulated a vast archive of social surveys. Some of which may be considered as big data. It was decided to do something similar to a repeated study. We wanted to see how universal the statistical law of a very high correlation between Likert means and yes % that Borg, Gabler noticed in 2002 was. How does this law hold in a different historical context, in a different culture, mea-suring a different (not workplace psychology) construct? If the repeated study could find identical or similar results, we would justifiably speak of a universal statistical law whose knowledge and application could help in the development of social survey statistical analyses and methodological culture.

2 Methods

The total sample contains 9 thousand subjects. The latter have been questioned in Lithuania (2016–2019) by standard survey techniques. A unified 5-grade Likert scale with graphical elements was used (Table 1). The survey asked citizens if they were satisfied/dissatisfied with public services.

The analysis was done on single items as well as on the level of psychometric scales. The large sample size is a result of the survey being given in 9 municipalities. The number of respondents in the separate samples (separate municipalities) reached 1 thousand subjects. The survey instrument was developed since 2002. It and its use can be found in [24].

Table 1. An example of a Likert scale Items used

EVALUATE	Very bad – very good				
Street management under critical weather conditions (freezing, strong winds)	.	.	●	●	●
Management of remote roads and drive-ways under critical weather conditions	.	.	●	●	●
Street, sidewalk, road repairs (road pit fixes, asphalting)	.	.	●	●	●
Road and street traffic sign condition	.	.	●	●	●
Street lighting during dark daytime	.	.	●	●	●
Evaluation categories	Disfavorable (Bad/Somewhat bad)		Neutral evaluation/ Don't know	Favorable(Somewhat good/Good)	
Evaluation encoding scores	1	2	3	4	5
Survey response scale	.	.	●	●	●

As is customary when a survey is done by public funds and for public needs, the reports of the applied study were (and still are) distributed freely on the internet [23]. They questionnaire contains around 190 primary variables which correspond to various indicators of public service: utilities, public transportation, environmental protection and recreation, education, culture, healthcare and social security, public safety and so on. Around 40 psychometric indices have been formed by logical and factor validation methods from services falling under a common theme, reflecting different areas of public service. The number of primary variables in every municipality questioned is almost identical. It may differ only by a few elements[1].

---

[1] For example, a particular urban centre does not contain a railway station and a hospital whose owner is the local government. Whereas the standard questionnaire includes questions on the railway station's environmental management and the services of a local hospital.

While looking for statistical dependencies it is important that the variables have a large variance. This condition is met. On a 190 variable list a natural clustering emerged. Some indicators tended to have positive evaluations and some negative, still others neutral. Out of a sample of 9 thousand a secondary database was formed consisting of 1695 items. It was composed of several variables: Likert scale means and agreement percentages of primary indicators, as well as disagreement and neutral evaluation percentages. The means of a Likert scale were defined by an independent variable - a predictor, while the "yes %" were defined by a dependent variable. Disagreement and neutral percentages were also defined as dependent variables.

Several research questions have been raised: what type of and how strong the statistical relation exists between the predictor and the dependent variables, that is between the means of primary Likert items and (a) Likert yes %; Likert no % and percentages falling under the "I have no opinion" category. The question of whether saturation of "I have no opinion" category has any impact on the strength between Likert means and yes % was also raised.

Accordingly, several main hypotheses were raised and tested:

1. There is a very strong correlation between Likert means and yes percentages approaching a linear dependence.
2. A large, saturated middle neutral category "I have no opinion" has a weak negative effect on the correlation between Likert means and "yes %".

3   Results

The means of both variables are distributed normally, both in the total sample and in the clusters of separate municipalities (Table 1, Figs. 1 and 2). It is to be expected by the central limit theorem as the sample size is large. However, the empirical distributions had to be tested. In the case of Kolmogorov-Smirnov test a natural paradox of large samples emerged: judging by the large K-S (two-tailed) significance test p-values, the normality of the sample is more strongly expressed in the separate municipality clusters rather than in the total sample. The p-value of the total sample is much smaller: for the Likert means $p = 0.052$ and in the case of yes % $p = 0.055$. Since the sample size was large, it was reasonable to ask for a large significance $p \leq 0.001$. In any case, skewness and kurtosis parameters have also been investigated. If the absolute values of these parameters do not cross 1.00, it is said by convention that the empirical distribution does not differ from the theoretical distribution significantly. Both in the total sample and in clusters small values of both parameters testify in favour of normality. Furthermore, as it should be, the total sample skewness and kurtosis parameters do not seem worse than the parameters of separate clusters.

There is a very strong linear relationship between the predictor and the dependent variable - yes % (Table 2, Figs. 3 and 4). $R^2 = 0.948$ for the total sample while for the 9 clusters it varies between $R^2 = 0.936$ and $R^2 = 0.968$. $p = .000$ in all cases.

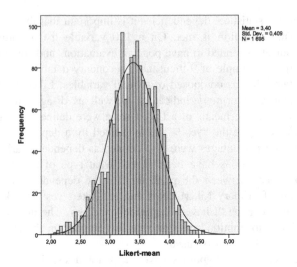

Fig. 1. Empirical distribution of Likert mean, N = 1695

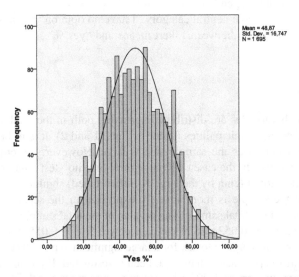

Fig. 2. Empirical distribution of agreement percentages (Yes %), N = 1695

It is symptomatic that the analogous relationship between Likert means and no% is clearly weaker. $R^2 = 0.865$ for the total sample and ranges from $R^2 = 0.772$ to $R^2 = 0.931$ for the 9 clusters, p = .000 in all cases. An even weaker relationship exists between Likert means and the neutral category "no opinion". $R^2 = 0,340$ for the total sample and in the 9 clusters ranges form $R^2 = 0,093$ to $R^2 = 0,622$, p = .000.

It became evident that increased saturation of the middle (neutral) category slightly weakens the relationship between Likert means and yes-%. The data corresponding to neutral evaluation frequencies were divided into groups by quartiles. The determination

Table 2. Normality tests of empirical distributions in different sample clusters and in the total sample; coefficients of determination R^2 (independent Variable- Means of Likert items, dependent variable - Yes %)

Sample	N_{sampl}	Value	K-S sig. (2 tailed)	Skewness	Kurtosis	R^2	p < 0.000
Sample 1 Ukmergė district	187	Likert mean	0,539	−0,383	0,254	0,940	****
		Yes %	0,819	0,140	−0,563		****
Sample 2 Radviliškis district	193	Likert mean	0,781	−0,188	−0,302	0,954	****
		Yes %	0,623	0,223	−0,58		****
Sample 3 Lazdijai district	190	Likert mean	0,077	−0,678	−0,302	0,951	****
		Yes %	0,738	−0,138	−0,693		****
Sample 4 Klaipėda reg. district	189	Likert mean	0,581	−0,313	−0,432	0,949	****
		Yes %	0,731	0,35	−0,887		****
Sample 5 Kedainiai district	189	Likert mean	0,794	−0,411	−0,061	0,950	****
		Yes %	0,600	0,069	−0,792		****
Sample 6 Druskininkai district	179	Likert mean	0,128	−0,408	0,223	0,958	****
		Yes %	0,058	−0,359	−0,554		****
Sample 7 Alytus district	181	Likert mean	0,176	−0,658	0,283	0,950	****
		Yes %	0,954	−0,142	−0,483		****
Sample 8 Jonava. district	195	Likert mean	0,983	−0,081	−0,243	0,968	****
		Yes %	0,870	0,123	−0,602		****
Sample 8 Jonava._2 district	192	Likert mean	0,945	0,046	−0,204	0,936	****
		Yes %	0,197	0,295	−0,603		****
Sample total	**1695**	Likert mean	**0,052**	**−0,327**	**0,054**	**0,948**	****
		Yes %	**0,055**	**0,057**	**−0,635**		****

coefficients of the first three quartiles are, respectively, $R^2 = 0.980$; $R^2 = 0.991$; $R^2 = 0.985$; they are large and close to each other. On the other hand the determination coefficient of the fourth quartile drops lower: $R^2 = 0.929$.

The fourth quartile contains the category "no opinion" which includes more than 39.1% of all frequencies. We are speaking of a rather large category of neutral answers. For reference, the various estimated parameters of neutral response frequencies: mean = 32.77; median = 32.8; mode = 31.5; min = 4.90; max = 60.40.

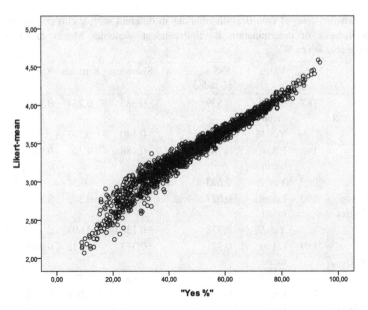

Fig. 3. Scatterplot (bivariat): independent Variable - Means of Likert items, dependent variable - Yes %), N = 1695

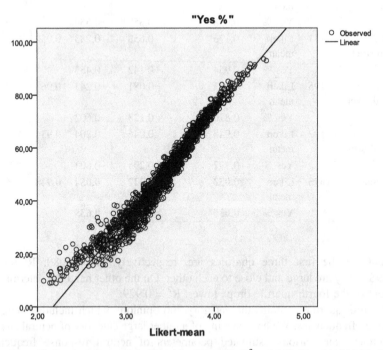

Fig. 4. Curve Estimation: Dependent Variable: "Yes %"; R^2 = 0,948; F = 31133,217, df1 = 1; df2 = 1693; p = 0,000; Parameter Estimates: Constant = −86,675; b1 = 39,857.

4   Conclusion and Discussion

There exists a very strong correlation between Likert means and Yes % which converges to a linear functional dependence. It means that these values correspond to the same underlying object. Thus, Yes % should take precedence since it has several advantages over Likert means. First of all, Yes % are more easily understood and interpreted. Second, there is no doubt over their mathematical "purity" whereas Likert means have problems: equal distances between scale orders are not guaranteed but postulated and the calculation of normal distribution parameters - mean and variance - from ordered data is not justified.

1. Correlation between Likert means and No % is palpably weaker. It shows that the Likert scale is not entirely symmetric, contrary to theoretical postulate. There exist some latent dependencies between stimulus-text comprehension and the preferences of answers. In the methodology of social attitude, measurement exists a textbook norm: if there is a long scale, it is necessary to formulate some statements positively and some negatively. Then it is likely that a randomization of semantic stimuli occurs which prevents any possible bias effects where, say, the respondents systematically start to pick "yes".
2. A very long category "no opinion" has a weak negative effect on the correlation between Likert mean and Yes %, even though the correlation still remains strong in general. This means that the modification of the Likert scale in which the researcher consciously decides to omit the neutral category "no opinion" does not necessarily imply a methodological opinion or error. It might sometimes be advantageous.
3. A question arose, why the correlation coefficient between the variables measured was slightly lower in this study than in the analogous Borg, Gabler study. Of course, we could rehabilitate the somewhat lower determination coefficient by hiding behind the confidence interval of the correlation coefficient. However, if the sample size is large enough, then the confidence interval is extremely small. Thus, we must take the fact at face value.

   It appears that the somewhat lower correlation between Likert mean and Yes % could have manifested as a side effect of this particular questionnaire and this particular sample. A hypothetical reason could be the high occurrence of "no opinion" answers. In the long and diverse list of public services some services are well known by the residents, their good or poor condition is seen by everyone (waste and environmental management, supply of drinking water, centralized heating) whereas some services are very specific and not encountered by everyone (services for the disabled, unemployed and so on). The "no opinion" answer for many specific services naturally rises in frequency. As has been shown, this slightly weakens the correlation. It is likely that if we had an instrument or a sample that did not have this systemic problem, then the correlation between Likert means and Yes % would be equally high as in Borg, Gabler study. It is simply necessary to have more data from repeated studies that would mitigate the possible side effects of a questionnaire or a sample.
4. This time the analysis was done only on the level of single items. The correlation between psychometric indices and average Yes % values on the scale was not

studied. It is worthwhile to do so in other studies, although it is not hard to guess that, given extremely high correlation on the primary items level, it will likewise repeat itself among additive psychometric indices.

5. It would be much more interesting to make an analogous repeated (or similar) study with 4–6 category Likert scale which does not include "no opinion" option. A no less meaningful analysis could be done with a 7 rank Likert scale that has a neutral category. A hypothesis would be that we should not expect any significant difference from Borg, Gabler or this study.

6. It is clear that social scientist who make survey reports to their colleague scientists, commissioners, consumers and media should use the Yes % more often and more widely rather than Likert means.

References

1. Balch, V.Ch.: Internet Survey Methodology. Cambridge Scholars Publishing, Tyne (2010)
2. Baros, W., Rost, J.: Natur-und kulturwissenschaftliche Perspektiven in der Psychologie. Methodologie, Methoden, Anwendungsbeispiele. Regener, Berlin (2012)
3. Borg, I., Gabler, S.: Zustimmungsanteile und Mittelwerte von Likertskalierten Items. ZUMA Nachrichten **26**(50), 7–25 (2002)
4. Bubelienė, D., Merkys, G.: School's cultural diversity: what is the difference between "school of happiness" and "school prison"? In: Lubkina, V., Danilane L., Usca, S. (eds.) International Scientific conference on Society, Integration, Education - SIE2019, vol. II, pp. 53–69. Rezekne Academy of Technologies, Rezekne (2019)
5. Carinio, J., Perla, R.J.: Ten common misunderstandings, misconceptions, persistent myths and urban legends about Likert scales and Likert response formats and their antidotes. J. Soc. Sci. **3**, 106–116 (2007)
6. Cunningham, W.A., Zelazo, P.D.: Attitudes and evaluations: a social cognitive neuroscience perspective. Trends Cogn. Sci. **11**(3), 97–104 (2007). https://doi.org/10.1016/j.tics.2006. 12.005
7. Dawes, J.: Do data characteristics change according to the number of scale points used? An experiment using 5-point, 7-point and 10-point scales. Int. J. Mark. Res. **50**(1), 61–77 (2008)
8. De Ayala, R.J.: The Theory and Practice of Item Response Theory. The Guilford Press, New York (2009)
9. Fischer, H.: A History of the Central Limit Theorem: From Classical to Modern Probability Theory. Springer, New York (2011)
10. Georgii, H.O.: Stochastik: Einführung in die Wahrscheinlichkeitstheorie und Statistik, vol. 4. de Gruyter, Auflage (2009)
11. Hambleton, R.K., Swaminathan, H., Rogers, H.J.: Fundamentals of Item Response Theory. Sage Press, Newbury Park (1991)
12. Heiberger, R.M., Robbins, N.B.: Design of diverging stacked bar charts for likert scales and other applications. J. Stat. Softw **57**(5), 1–32 (2014)
13. Hofmans, J.: Editorial: applications of functional measurement in psychology. Psichologica **31**(3), 431–439 (2010)
14. Hofmans, J., Theuns, P., Mairesse, O.: Impact of the number of response categories on linearity and sensivity of self-anchoring scales. Methdology **3**(4), 160–169 (2007)
15. Jacoby, J., Matell, M.S.: Three-point likert scales are good enough. J. Mark. Res. **8**(4), 495–500 (1971)

16. Jamieson, S.: Likert scales: how to (ab)use them. Med. Educ. **38**(12), 1217–1218 (2004)
17. Kanai, R., Feilden, T., Firth, C., Rees, G.: Political orientations are correlated with brain structure in young adults. Curr. Biol. **21**(8), 677–680 (2011)
18. Kemper, Ch., Brähler, E. Zenger, M.: Psychologische und sozialwissenschaftliche Kurzskalen. Standardisierte Erhebungsinstrumente für Wissenschaft und Praxis. Medizinisch Wissechaftliche Verlagsgesellschaft, Berlin (2014)
19. Lamnek, S., Krell, C.: Qualitative Sozialforschung 6., überarbeitete Auflage. Beltz Verlag, Weinheim (2016)
20. Likert, R.: A technique for the measurement of attitudes. Arch. Psychol. **22**(140), 55 (1932)
21. Lozano, L.M., Carcia-Cueto, E., Muniz, J.: Effect of the number of response categories on the reliability and validity of rating scales. Methdology **4**(2), 73–79 (2008)
22. Merkys, G., Bagdonas, A., Bubelienė, D.: Vaiko ir mokyklos saugumo vertinimo klausimynas: indikatoriai ir faktorinė validacija. Socialinis ugdymas **3**(35), 52–61 (2013)
23. Merkys, G., Bubelienė, D.: Radviliškio rajono savivaldybė "Radviliškio rajono gyventojų pasitenkinimo viešosiomis paslaugomis apskaičiavimo indeksas" (2017). (Unprinted report). http://www.radviliskis.lt/lit/Ar-radviliskio-rajono-gyventojai-patenkinti-teikiamomis-viesosiomis-paslaugomis-kvieciame-susipazinti-su-tyrimo-ataskaita
24. Merkys, G., Brazienė, R.: Evaluation of public services provided by municipalities in Lithuania: an experience of applying a standardized survey inventory. Soc. Sci. **4**(66), 50–61 (2009)
25. Rost, J.: Lehrbuch Testtheorie - Testkonstruktion (2., vollst. überarb. u. erw. Aufl.). Bern, Huber (2004)
26. Steyer, R., Schmitt, M., Eid, M.: Latent state-trait theory and research in personality and individual differences. Eur. J. Pers. **3**, 389–408 (1999)

Modeling and Analysis of Social-Behavioral Processes

Modeling and Simulation of Impact and Control in Social Networks

M. T. Agieva[1], A. V. Korolev[2], and G. A. Ougolnitsky[3(✉)]

[1] Ingush State University, Nazran, Russian Federation
agieva25@mail.ru
[2] Saint Petersburg Higher School of Economics,
Saint Petersburg, Russian Federation
danitschi@gmail.com
[3] Southern Federal University, Rostov-on-Don, Russian Federation
ougoln@mail.ru

Abstract. The problems of analysis and prediction in social networks are interpreted for the domain of marketing (other applications are also possible). Algorithms of determination of the strong subgroups and satellites for a network are implemented using the programming language R and tested on model examples. An original algorithm of calculation of the final opinions is proposed, implemented in R and also tested on the model examples. The main idea is that all control efforts in marketing (and other problem domains) should be directed only to the members of strong subgroups because they and only they determine the final opinions of all members of the network. Based on this idea, two problems of the opinions control on networks are studied. First, a static game in normal form where the players maximize the final opinions of all members of a target audience by means of the marketing impact to the initial opinions of some members of the strong subgroups. Second, a dynamic (difference) game in normal form where the players solve the problem of maximization of the sum of opinions of the members of a target audience by means of the closed-loop strategies of impact to the current opinions of the members of strong subgroups. In both cases we received the analytical solutions and conducted their comparative analysis. More complicated versions of the models are studied numerically on the base of the method of qualitatively representative scenarios in computer simulation.

Keywords: Computer simulation · Difference games · Optimal control theory · Social networks

1 Introduction

The first model of influence in a social group was suggested by French [1] and Harary [2] and considered in detail by De Groot [3]. Later on, numerous extensions and refinements of this model were studied by different researchers, namely, the case of

---

The work is supported by the Russian Science Foundation, project #17-19-01038.

N. Agarwal et al. (Eds.): MSBC 2019, CCIS 1079, pp. 29–40, 2019.
https://doi.org/10.1007/978-3-030-29862-3_3

time-varying mutual influence in [4–6], the convergence conditions of opinions in [7–9], the rate of convergence in [4, 9], and the uniqueness conditions of a resulting opinion in [4, 5].

In [10] the Markovian model of influence in a group was represented as a dynamic Bayesian network of two-level structure (separate individuals and the whole group). This model has a close connection to the series of models from the same class, i.e., the mixed memory Markov model [11], the implicit paired Markovian model [12], and dynamical systems trees [13].

For a most comprehensive study of network modeling, see the monograph by Jackson [14] and also the paper [15]. Communication and coordination in social networks were analyzed in [16]. The papers [17–19] are dedicated to the modeling of word-of-mouth. The relative influence of network nodes was investigated in [20]. A systems approach to networks was given in [21]. The network models of social influence were also described in [22, 23].

A detailed treatment of influence models and some statements of control problems over networks were presented in the monograph [24]. The authors introduced a classification of such models using a system of effects and properties of the social networks as follows: individual opinions of agents; variable opinions under an influence of other network members; different significance of opinions (influence, trust) of given agents for other agents; different degrees of the agent's susceptibility to influence (conformity, stability of opinions); opinion leaders (agents with maximal influence); a threshold of sensitivity to the opinion variations of a neighborhood; local groups (by interests, by close opinions); social correlation factors; less significant external factors of influence (advertising, marketing events) and external agents (mass media, product suppliers, etc.); stages—typical phases of opinion dynamics for social network members (e.g., diffusion of innovations); avalanche-like effects (cascades); the influence of structural properties of the social networks on opinion dynamics; optimization of informational influence. Opinion dynamics was studied in a series of typical examples. Control problems were stated and some results on linear models were obtained.

The closest approach is presented in [25, 26] where linear-quadratic game theoretic models on a network with two influence nodes are built and investigated. In [25] a Nash equilibrium for the independent influence nodes is found, while in [26] the nodes are hierarchically ordered and a Stackelberg equilibrium is calculated.

There are also many different approaches to the modeling and simulation of networks, including such methods as gene-environment networks, eco-finance networks, rumor propagation, Markov switching models and others. A comprehensive survey is given in [27] where presented advances achieved during the last years in the development and use of operations research, in particular, optimization methods in the new gene-environment and eco-finance networks, based on usually finite data series, with an emphasis on uncertainty in them and in the interactions of the model items. The networks represent models in the form of time-continuous and time-discrete dynamics, whose unknown parameters are estimated under constraints on complexity and regularization by various kinds of optimization techniques, ranging from linear, mixed-integer, spline, semi-infinite and robust optimization to conic, e.g., semi-definite programming. Different kinds of uncertainties and a new time-discretization technique are presented, some aspects of data preprocessing and stability, related aspects from game theory and financial mathematics are described.

The paper [28] surveys and improves recent advances in understanding the foundations and interdisciplinary implications of the newly introduced gene–environment networks, and it integrates the important theme of carbon dioxide emission reduction into the networks and dynamics. Some operational and managerial issues of practical working and decision making, expressed in terms of sliding windows, quadrants (modules) of parametric effects, and navigating (controlling) between such effects and directing them are introduced and investigated by nonlinear ordinary differential equations that contain parameters that have to be determined. For this, modern (Chebychevian) approximation and (generalized semi-infinite) optimization are used. After this is provided, time-discretized dynamical systems are studied. A combinatorial algorithm with polyhedral sequences allows to detect the region of parametric stability. The authors of [29] consider dynamical gene-environment networks under ellipsoidal uncertainty and discuss the corresponding set-theoretic regression models. Clustering techniques are applied for an identification of functionally related groups of genes and environmental factors. The uncertain states of cluster elements are represented in terms of ellipsoids referring to stochastic dependencies between the multivariate data variables. The time-dependent behavior of the system variables and clusters is determined by a regulatory system with (affine-) linear coupling rules. Explicit representations of the uncertain multivariate future states of the system are calculated by ellipsoidal calculus. Various set-theoretic regression models are introduced in order to estimate the unknown system parameters.

Eco-finance networks under uncertainty are discussed in [30]. A mathematical model described the propagation of information including rumor and truth is presented in [31]. An existence of the equilibria, local stability and global asymptotical stability, and the propagation threshold of rumor spreading are investigated. Numerical simulation is made to demonstrate the results.

Markov switching models were applied to the economic analysis in [32]. They have become increasingly popular in economic studies of industrial production, interest rates, stock prices and unemployment rates. Markov switching models are often adopted by researchers wishing to account for specific features of economic time series such as the asymmetry of economic activity over the business cycle or the fat tails, volatility clustering and mean reversion in stock prices and interest rates. These features translate into the higher-order moments and serial correlation of the data-generating process, so a characterization of the moments and autocorrelation function generated by Markov switching will allow researchers to better understand when to make use of this class of models. The contribution of the paper [33] is to characterize the moments and serial correlation of the level and the squared values of Markov switching processes. The authors of [34] study a stochastic optimal control problem for a delayed Markov regime-switching jump-diffusion model and establish necessary and sufficient maximum principles under full and partial information for such a system. They prove the existence–uniqueness theorem for the adjoint equations represented by an anticipated backward stochastic differential equation with jumps.

The paper [35] treats boundary value problems on large periodic networks which arise in many applications such as soil mechanics in geophysics or the analysis of photonic crystals in nanotechnology. As a model example, singularly perturbed elliptic differential equations of second order are addressed. In modern material sciences and multi-scale physics homogenization approaches provide a global characterization of physical systems that depend on the topology of the underlying microgeometry. Purely formal approaches such as averaging techniques can be applied for an identification of the averaged system. For models in variational form, two-scale convergence for network functions can be used to derive the homogenized model. The sequence of solutions of the variational microcsopic models and the corresponding sequence of tangential gradients converge toward limit functions that are characterized by the solution of the variational macroscopic model. In [36] further extension of this result is proved. The variational macroscopic model can be equivalently represented by a homogenized model on the superior domain and a certain number of reference cell problems. In this way, the results obtained by averaging strategies are supported by notions of convergence for network functions on varying domains. In [37], the authors integrate the data uncertainty of real-world models into regulatory systems and robustify them. They newly introduce and analyze robust time-discrete target–environment regulatory systems under polyhedral uncertainty through robust optimization.

The aim of [38] is to provide a mathematical framework for studying node cooperation, and to define strategies leading to optimal node behavior in ad hoc networks. The authors show time performances of three different methods, namely, Dijkstra's algorithm, Dijkstra's algorithm with battery times and cooperative flow game algorithm constructed from a flow network model. There are two main outcomes of the study regarding the shortest path problem which is that of finding a path of minimum length between two distinct vertices in a network. The first one finds out which method gives better results in terms of time while finding the shortest path, the second one considers the battery life of wireless devices on the network to determine the remaining nodes on the network. Further, optimization performances of the methods are examined in finding the shortest path problem. The study shows that the battery times play an important role in network routing and more devices provided to keep the network. Also, considering the cooperation between the nodes, it is envisaged that using cooperative game theory brings a new approach to network traffic engineering and routing methods.

Contribution of this paper includes the following. The problems of analysis and prediction in social networks are interpreted for the domain of marketing. Other applications are also possible [39]. Algorithms of determination of the strong subgroups and satellites for a network are implemented using the programming language R [40] and tested on model examples. An original algorithm of calculation of the final opinions is proposed, implemented in R and also tested on the model examples. The main idea is that all control efforts in marketing (and other problem domains) should be directed only to the members of strong subgroups because they and only they determine the final opinions of all members of the network. The respective optimal control and difference games problem statements are given and studied both analytically and numerically on the base of the method of qualitatively representative scenarios in computer simulation [41].

Section 2 describes the basic model of influence in a social group, including its marketing interpretation, as well as formulates associated analysis and prediction problems. Section 3 is dedicated to optimization and game-theoretic models of conflict control taking network specifics into account. The results are summarized in the Sect. 4.

2 Analysis and Prediction Problems

Following [42], consider the basic model of influence in a social group based on Markov chains. A group of n members $y_1, \ldots, y_n$ has to make a decision about an issue. At the initial time $t = 0$, each member y_i has an opinion $x_i(0)$ on this issue; the vector of opinions $x^0 = x(0) = (x_1(0), \ldots, x_n(0))$ is given. Denote by $a_{ij} \geq 0$ the degree of influence of y_i on y_j (equivalently, the degree of trust of y_j to y_i). Generally the values a_{ij} can be called the coefficients of interaction within the group. The interaction within the group is formalized by an influence directed graph $D = (Y, A)$, $Y = \{y_1, \ldots, y_n\}$, $A = \|a_{ij}\|_{i,j=1}^{n}$. Introduce the following assumptions: D remains invariable in the course of decision-making; all decisions are made at the discrete moments of time $t = 0, 1, 2, \ldots$; the opinions of group members evolve in accordance with the rule

$$x_j(t+1) = \sum_{i=1}^{n} a_{ij} x_i(t), \quad j = 1, \ldots, n.$$

Then the following questions arise.

(i) Does there exist a stable resulting opinion $x_i^{\infty} = \lim_{t \to \infty} x_i(t)$ for each group member?

(ii) Will the whole group reach the same stable resulting opinion $x^{\infty} = x_i^{\infty}$, $i = 1, \ldots, n$?

A set of nodes $\{y_1, \ldots, y_k\}$ of an influence digraph $D = (Y, A)$ is called *a strong subgroup* if it represents a strong component of D that enters the node base of its condensation $D*$. Other nodes are called *satellites*. It is shown [42] that:

- the resulting opinion of any member of a strong subgroup depends only on the initial opinions of its other members, being the same for the whole subgroup;
- the resulting opinion of any satellite depends on the opinions of all strong subgroups members but not on the opinions of other satellites. The resulting opinion is the weighted average of the common resulting opinions of all strong subgroups.

Thus, influence models over networks can be used for solving analysis and prediction problems. The former class of problems includes identification of strong subgroups and satellites as well as calculation of some indicators of the network. The latter class of problems is focused on predicting the opinion dynamics of social group members based on its structure identified in the course of analysis. Table 1 gives an interpretation of different elements of these models in marketing.

Consider a model example which illustrates such a wide spread kind of activity in social networks as blogging. The nodes represent five ladies with small children supporting the blogs about beauty, health, and maternity (nodes 1-5) as well as their

Table 1. Models of influence and control in social networks: Interpretation of different elements in marketing.

Model element	Mathematical sense	Marketing interpretation
Basic agent	Network node	Segment of audience
Influencing agent	Network node	Market participants (firms), advertising agencies, mass media
Opinion of basic agent	Real value associated with each node (basic agent) that varies in time	Agent's monthly (annual) expenses on firm's products
Trust (influence)	Arc between initial and terminal nodes	Word-of-mouth, other communications of agents
Degree of trust of basic agent to another one	Real value associated with each network arc	Quantitative characteristic of trust
Resulting opinion	Limit value of opinion over infinite time horizon	Stable resulting opinion over long period of time
Strong subgroup	Non-degenerate strong component of the network correspondent to an ergodic set	Determines its own resulting opinions and also the dependent opinions of other agents
Satellite	Subset of nodes representing degenerate strong components	Resulting opinions are completely determined by strong subgroups
Influence on opinions	Additive term of opinion vector (more complex cases are possible)	Marketing action plan
Impact on degrees of trust (influence)	Additive term of influence matrix (more complex cases are possible)	Marketing action plan
Goal of control	Domain in the state space of a network	Range of desired opinions

followers who discuss the price of prams (opinions). Take a digraph with 100 nodes and calculate some characteristics of the social network. It is evident that the only strong subgroup is formed by the bloggers, and their followers are satellites (Figs. 1 and 2). The situation with the indicators of centrality is similar: the bloggers have a power on their followers who trust them (Fig. 3).

An original algorithm of the solution of the prediction problem (calculation of the final opinions) is developed and implemented in the programming language R [40]. The most complicated part of the algorithm is its embedded cycle with depth two. So, the complexity of the algorithm is equal to $O(n^2)$, where n is a number of nodes. This complexity is acceptable for the graphs with a big enough number of nodes. The algorithm is also tested on the model example described above. The bloggers have a decisive influence of their direct followers and other members of the network. Thus, it is more rational to address the advertisement of trams to the five bloggers than to hundreds of their followers.

Fig. 1. Bloggers and their followers: a social network.

Fig. 2. Strong subgroups and satellites.

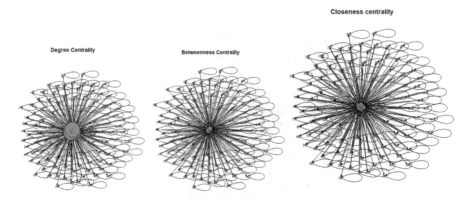

Fig. 3. Indicators of centrality.

3 Optimization and Game Theoretic Control Problems

The main idea about control in this context is that all marketing efforts should be directed only to the members of strong subgroups because they and only they determine the final opinions of all members of the network. Suppose that the strong subgroups are determined in the previous stage of analysis described above. We have investigated analytically two conflict control problems. First, a static game theoretic model in normal form of increasing the final opinions of the members of target audience by the marketing impact to the initial opinions of some members of the strong subgroups.

Second, a dynamic (difference) game theoretic model in normal form of maximization of the sum of opinions of the members of target audience by the marketing impact in close-loop strategies to the current opinions of the members of strong subgroups.

In both problems the independent and cooperative behavior of the players is considered, the solutions are received in the explicit form, and the comparative analysis is conducted. Thus, the ratio of optimal solutions in the cases of cooperative (u^C) and independent (u^N) behavior is

$$\frac{u^C}{u^N} = \sqrt[p]{\frac{R \sum\limits_{i,j:h(i,j,k)=1} [w_j^{(i)}]^{\frac{p}{p-1}}}{R_k \sum\limits_{k=1}^{m} \sum\limits_{i,j:h(i,j,k)=1} [w_j^{(i)}]^{\frac{p}{p-1}}}},$$

where R_k, R - the marketing budget of the k-th firm and the total marketing budget respectively, $w_j^{(i)}$ - a component of the stationary vector of the Markov chain for the i-th strong subgroup and the j-th agent, $p > 0$ - a model parameter. From one side, in the case of cooperation the marketing efforts decrease because there are more firms and they in fact advertise the same product. From the other side, the efforts can increase because the total marketing budget in the case of cooperation is greater.

Also, the non-linear model of optimal control

$$J = \sum_{t=1}^{T} e^{-\rho t} \left[\sum_{j=1}^{n} x_j^t - \sum_{k=1}^{m} u_k^t \right] \rightarrow \max; \quad \sum_{t=1}^{T} \sum_{j=1}^{m} e^{-\rho t} u_j^t \leq R;$$

$$x_j^{t+1} = b_j \sqrt{u_j^t} + \sum_{i=1}^{n} a_{ij} x_i^t, \; x_j^0 = x_{j0}, \; j = 1, \ldots, n, \; t = 0, 1, \ldots, T$$

was investigated numerically by means of the simulation modeling. Therefore, the models of influence and control in social groups have several applications in marketing (see Table 2).

Table 2. Models of influence and control over networks and their applications to marketing.

Model problems	Applications to marketing
Network analysis	1. Audience segmentation, identification of strong subgroups that determine the inner common resulting opinions of subgroups members and also the individual resulting opinions of other agents (satellites) as a linear combination of resulting opinions of strong subgroups 2. Calculation of centrality, prestige and other characteristics of the audience
Prediction	Calculation of resulting opinions of all agents without external impact
Optimal control	Choice of optimal marketing actions (impact) for the audience by one firm
Dynamic games	Choice of compromise impact on the audience in the case of competition and/or cooperation of firms (in the latter case, taking into account the homeostasis conditions, e.g., limited consumption)

4 Conclusions

Social networks are a popular object for the mathematical modeling and simulation since the second half of the past century. There are many different approaches to their modeling and simulation which use diverse mathematical techniques, both discrete and continuous, deterministic and stochastic ones. Among them it is possible to differentiate the gene-environment models, eco-finance models, rumor propagation models, Markov switching models as well as graph theoretic models and methods of optimal control and game theory. In total, they give a comprehensive description of the network dynamics.

This paper develops the De Groot model and presents problem statements for analysis, prediction, optimal and conflict control in social groups with a given network structure of interactions. These statements have been interpreted by an example of the target groups (audience) in marketing.

At the structural analysis stage, an audience is segmented into strong subgroups and satellites. The initial opinions of strong subgroups members determine the common resulting opinions of each such subgroup and also the individual resulting opinions of satellites, which actually solves the opinion prediction problem. Algorithms of determination of the strong subgroups and satellites for a network are implemented using the programming language R and tested on model examples. An original algorithm of calculation of the final opinions is proposed, implemented in R and also tested on the model examples.

A natural extension is the formulation and solution of optimal and conflict (game-theoretic) control problems (how to change the final opinions in a desired direction). The above-mentioned result describes the specifics of these problems as follows: one or several control subjects should exert impact only on the opinions of the members of strong subgroups and the coefficients of their interaction with other agents. The optimal and/or conflict control problems can be supplemented by the homeostasis condition, which specifies social (public) requirements to an active system under control. Generally, these requirements contradict the direct economic interests of control subjects and hence can be included into the control problem statement with a voluntary self-restraint of control subjects (social responsibility) or a special control subject maintaining homeostasis by compulsion or impulsion of other control subjects. The latter variant leads to the consideration of hierarchical dynamic games with phase constraints.

It is supposed to continue the investigation for the cases of independent, hierarchically ordered, and cooperative control subjects for different non-linear control impacts. It is also interesting to consider natural uncertainty.

References

1. French, J.R.: A formal theory of social power. Psychol. Rev. **63**, 181–194 (1956)
2. Harary, F.: A criterion for unanimity in French's theory of social power, in studies in social power, pp. 168–182. Institute of Sociological Research, Michigan (1959)
3. De Groot, M.H.: Reaching a consensus. J. Am. Stat. Assoc. **69**, 118–121 (1974)
4. Golub, B., Jackson, M.: Naive learning in social networks and the wisdom of crowds. Am. Econ. J.: Microecon. **2**(1), 112–149 (2010)
5. Hegselman, R., Krause, U.: Opinion dynamics and bounded confidence models: analysis and simulation. J. Artif. Soc. Soc. Simul. **5**(3) (2002)
6. Krause, U.: A discrete nonlinear and non-autonomous model of consensus formation. In: Communications in Difference Equations. Amsterdam: Gordon and Breach Publishers, pp. 227–236 (2000)
7. Berger, R.J.: A necessary and sufficient conditions for reaching a consensus using De Groot's method. J. Am. Stat. Assoc. **76**, 415–419 (1981)
8. Chatterjee, S., Seneta, E.: Toward consensus: some convergence theorems on repeated averaging. J. Appl. Probab. **14**, 159–164 (1977)
9. De Marzo, P., Vayanos, D., Zwiebel, J.: Persuasion bias, social influence and unidimensional opinions. Quart. J. Econ. **118**(3), 909–968 (2003)
10. Zhang, D., Gatica-Perez, D., Bengio, S., Roy, D.: Learning influence among interactive markov chains. In: Neural Information Processing Systems (NIPS), pp. 132–141 (2005)

11. Saul, L.K., Jordan, M.I.: Mixed memory markov models: decomposing complex stochastic processes as mixtures of simpler ones. Mach. Learn. **37**(1), 75–87 (1999)
12. Oliver, N., Rosario, B., Pentland, A.: Graphical models for recognizing human interactions. In: Neural Information Processing Systems (NIPS), pp. 924–930 (1998)
13. Howard, A., Jebara, T.: Dynamical systems trees. In: Uncertainty in Artificial Intelligence, pp. 260–267 (2003)
14. Jackson, M.: Social and Economic Networks. Princeton University Press, Princeton (2008)
15. Jackson, M., Wolinsky, A.: A strategic model of social and economic networks. J. Econ. Theory **71**(1), 44–74 (1996)
16. Chwe, M.S.: Communication and coordination in social networks. Rev. Econ. Stud. **67**, 1–16 (2000)
17. Buttle, F.A.: Word-of-mouth: understanding and managing referral marketing. J. Strategic Mark. **6**, 241–254 (1998)
18. Godes, D., Mayzlin, D.: Using online conversations to study word of mouth communication. Mark. Sci. **23**, 545–560 (2004)
19. Goldenberg, J., Libai, B., Muller, E.: Talk of the network: a complex systems look at the underlying process of word-of-mouth. Mark. Lett. **2**, 11–34 (2001)
20. Masuda, N., Kawamura, Y., Kori, H.: Analysis of relative influence of nodes in directed networks. Phys. Rev. **E80**, 046114 (2009)
21. Newman, M.: The structure and function of complex networks. SIAM Rev. **45**(2), 167–256 (2003)
22. Robins, G., Pattison, P., Elliot, P.: Network models for social influence processes. Psychometrica **66**(2), 161–190 (2001)
23. Watts, D.: The, "New" Science of Networks. Ann. Rev. Sociol. **30**, 243–270 (2004)
24. Chkhartishvili, A., Gubanov, D., Novikov, D.: Social Networks: Models of Information Influence, Control, and Confrontation. Springer, Heielberg (2019). https://doi.org/10.1007/978-3-030-05429-8
25. Sedakov, A., Zhen, M.: Opinion dynamics game in a social network with two influence nodes. Appl. Math. Inform. Control process. **15**(1), 118–125 (2019). Vestnik SPbGU
26. Zhen, M.: Stackelberg equilibrium in opinion dynamics game in social network with two influence nodes. In: Petrosyan, L., Zenkevich, N. (eds.) Contributions to Game Theory and Management. Vol. XII. Collected papers presented on the Twelfth International Conference Game Theory and Management, pp. 366–386. SPb., Saint Petersburg State University (2019)
27. Alparslan-Gok, S.Z., Defterli, O., Kropat, E., Weber, G.-W.: Modeling, inference and optimization of regulatory networks based on time series data. Eur. J. Oper. Res. **211**(1), 1–14 (2011)
28. Alparslan-Gok, S.Z., Soyler, B., Weber, G.-W.: A new mathematical approach in environmental and life sciences: gene-environment networks and their dynamics. Environ. Model. Assess. **14**(2), 267–288 (2009)
29. Belen, S., Kropat, E., Weber, G.-W.: Dynamical gene-environment networks under ellipsoidal uncertainty: set-theoretic regression analysis based on ellipsoidal OR. In: Dynamics, Games and Science I: DYNA 2008, Honor of Maurício Peixoto and David Rand, University of Minho, Braga, Portugal, 8–12 September, pp. 545–571 (2008)
30. Kropat, E., Weber, G.-W., Akteke-Ozturk, B.: Eco-finance networks under uncertainty. In: Herskovits, J., Canelas, A., Cortes, H., Aroztegui, M. (eds.) Proceedings of the International Conference on Engineering Optimization, Rio de Janeiro, Brazil (2008)
31. Liu, Y.J., Zeng, C.M., Luo, Y.Q.: Dynamics of a new rumor propagation model with the spread of truth. Appl. Math. **9**, 536–549 (2018)

32. Hamilton, J.D.: A new approach to the economic analysis of nonstationary time series and the business cycle. Econometrica **57**, 357–384 (1989)
33. Timmermann, A.: Moments of Markov switching models. J. Econ. **96**, 75–111 (2000)
34. Savku, E., Weber, G.-W.: A stochastic maximum principle for a markov regime-switching jump-diffusion model with delay and an application to finance. J. Optim. Theory Appl. **179**(2), 696–721 (2018)
35. Kropat, E., Meyer-Nieberg, S., Weber, G.-W.: Singularly perturbed diffusion-advection-reaction processes on extremely large three-dimensional curvilinear networks with a periodic microstructure: efficient solution strategies based on homogenization theory. Numer. Algebra **6**(2), 183–219 (2016)
36. Kropat, E., Meyer-Nieberg, S., Weber, G.-W.: Bridging the gap between variational homogenization results and two-scale asymptotic averaging techniques on periodic network structures. Numer. Algebra **7**(3), 223–250 (2017)
37. Kropat, E., Ozmen, A., Weber, G.-W.: Robust optimization in spline regression models for multi-model regulatory networks under polyhedral uncertainty. Optimization **66**(12), 2135–2155 (2017)
38. Alparslan-Gok, S.Z., Aydogan, T., Ergun, S., Weber, G.-W.: Performance analysis of a cooperative flow game algorithm in ad hoc networks and a comparison to Dijkstra's algorithm. J. Ind. Manage. Optim. **15**(3), 1085–1100 (2019)
39. Agieva, M.T., Ougolnitsky, G.A.: Regional sustainable management problems on networks. In: Russkova, E. (ed.) Proceedings of the International Scientific Conference "Competitive, Sustainable and Secure Development of the Regional Economy: Response to Global Challenges" (CSSDRE 2018). Advances in Economics, Business and Management Research (AEBMR), vol. 39, pp. 6–9. Atlantis Press (2018). https://doi.org/10.2991/cssdre-18.2018.2
40. Kabacoff, R.: R in Action: Data analysis and graphics with R. Manning Publications, Shelter Island (2011)
41. Ougolnitsky, G.A., Usov, A.B.: Computer simulations as a solution method for differential games. In: Pfeffer, M.D., Bachmaier, E. (eds.) Computer Simulations: Advances in Research and Applications, pp. 63–106. Nova Science Publishers, New York (2018)
42. Roberts, F.: Discrete Mathematical Models with Applications to Social, Biological and Environmental Problems. Prentice-Hall, Upper Saddle River (1976)

Finding Fake News Key Spreaders in Complex Social Networks by Using Bi-Level Decomposition Optimization Method

Mustafa Alassad[(✉)], Muhammad Nihal Hussain,
and Nitin Agarwal[(✉)]

University of Arkansas, Little Rock, AR, USA
{mmalassad, mnhussain, nxagarwal}@ualr.edu

Abstract. Focal structure analysis explores the smallest possible sets of individuals can influence maximum number of users in social networks. These sets of individuals, when coordinating together, maximize information diffusing, influencing operations, or mobilizing crowds. Focal structure sets have enough resources at their disposal to regulate the flow of information in the network. Due to drawbacks in general Node-based and group-based community detection algorithms, these small influential sets are not discovered, and they remain hidden or forgotten in large communities. In this research, we propose a two-level decomposition optimization method to discover these intensive groups in complex social networks. We utilized a two-level decomposition problem maximizing the influencer nodes and the network's global sparsity/modularity measures, subjected to small real-world network metrics. Later, we demonstrate the efficacy of our model by applying it to a YouTube network. The dataset was collected by identifying a YouTube channel that had more than 15 million views and was spreading fake news or conspiracy theory videos related to the conflict in the South China Sea. The dataset consisted of 47,265 comments on 5,095 videos by 8,477 commenters. We applied focal structure analysis to co-commenter network, where two commenters were connected if they commented on the same video, to identify the sets of individuals that are coordinating to manipulate YouTube's recommendation algorithm to maximize the spread of fake news. The proposed method in this research identified the smallest entities that had high influence, interactions, and higher reachability for information dissemination. Also, a multi-criteria optimization problem is deployed to rank the identified sets for in-depth explorations.

Keywords: Social network analysis · Focal structure analysis · Fake news spreaders · Bi-level optimization · Multi-criteria optimization method

1 Introduction

With Social media platforms being used as powerful democratization tools to mobilize crowds during various global events like "The Arab Spring", "Egyptian Revolution", "Yellow Vests Movement" and other "Occupy Movements" worldwide, there is an

N. Agarwal et al. (Eds.): MSBC 2019, CCIS 1079, pp. 41–54, 2019.
https://doi.org/10.1007/978-3-030-29862-3_4

increase in interest to identify influencers that can spread information and motivate to participate in these events. Where any user can influence based on his/her ability to disseminate interesting content, ideas, belief to other people, or initiate an interesting discussion [1], huge events require multiple nodes that can influence and coordinate the network.

Researchers have developed several methods for detecting clusters in the complex networks such as modularity method, where it might skip the hidden small important patterns in the network [2, 3]. Exploring and finding such forgotten groups is imperative. Therefore, in this research we seek to identify key sets of individuals that can influence top number of users in the network, instead of finding regular communities or influential users in social networks, this research identifies the focal groups using Focal Structure Analysis (FSA) approach.

The problem with algorithms that identify the influential nodes is that they are focused only on the node level aspects and measure node's resources, power, and opportunities. Also, the same gap is available with the community algorithms, where they ignore the node level aspects. This study bridges the gap and uses both node level and network level aspects to identify focal groups, as shown in Fig. 1.

Focal structure analysis is the identification of sets of individuals in social network that may or may not be influential on their own but are influential collectively [4]. Sen et al. [5], identified the method of the focal structure by utilizing a greedy algorithm for discovering influential sets of individuals. The author's algorithm was based on local and global structures and was able to find the atomic intensive groups in social networks. But the model suffered from some major drawbacks such as chain sets having zero average clustering coefficient values were identified as focal groups, and the model limited the central nodes by assigning each node to only one set.

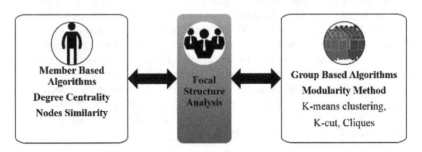

Fig. 1. Focal structure analysis is a mix of two network analysis algorithms, i.e., identifying authoritative individuals and identifying communities.

In this paper, we propose a model to search for sets smaller than the regular communities identified by group-based category and at the same time they should include influential nodes identified by the left side algorithms as shown in Fig. 1. For this purpose, we considered a bi-level linear optimization problem that can solve the above problem. The bi-level algorithm considers node-level aspects for measuring the node's degree centrality and average clustering coefficient values, and the network-level aspects to evaluate the global impacts or modularity values.

In the next step, we implemented real-world small network metrics [6] to evaluate the identified sets and utilized a multi-criteria optimization model to rank the focal structure sets for further investigations. We also, demonstrate the efficiency of the proposed algorithm by applying it to a network of commenters on YouTube channel that had more than 15 million views and was spreading fake news or conspiracy theory videos related to the conflict in the South China Sea. The dataset was curated using the methodology explained by Hussain et al. [7].

The rest of the paper is organized as follows. First, a few extant literatures on influencers and community detection algorithms are reviewed. Next, the empirical study is described, and the findings are discussed. Lastly, we discuss conclusions, limitations, and ideas for future works.

2 Related Works

The fields of graph theory, network science, and network analysis have been extensively studied. Researchers have found various node level measures as well as network level measures to identify various aspects of the network.

Influence of Influencer users in social networks can be calculated based on their ability to disseminate interesting content, ideas, beliefs to other people, or initiate an interesting discussion [1]. Likewise, the PageRank [8], and HITS [9] can find the authoritative users in social networks, where a central node connects many other nodes and a central node is connected by many other users.

The users' ability to disseminated information has been investigated in many researches such as Herzig et al. [10, 11] where the authors studied the problem of detecting topic based influences in social media. Briscoe et al. [12] encountered the truthfulness of information from unknown sources in online platforms. The authors determined the credibility in ego-centric network's by utilizing the degree centrality and geodesic distance. Jones and O'Neill [13] studied the exchange of information and content between different groups of users considering their various relationships. The authors concluded that similarity between the sets created by users and those created by the algorithm is correlated with the modularity of their network. Measuring the individual's power and opportunities based on the node position inside the network structure would help to find the prominent nodes that have the most influences to their neighbors [14–21].

Scientists in graph theory applied many algorithms to maximize the modularity of the network. Network clustering applied by Newman [22] proposed an effective method to cluster the network into smoother subgraphs. Optimizing the modularity value is an NP-hard problem [23], and in this domain, various applications are available to maximize any graph modularity value [24–30].

3   Proposed Methodology

Since the model proposed by Sen et al. [5] suffered from drawback such as explored chain sets and assigning each node to only one set, we implemented a Bi-Level decomposition model to identify small intensive sets. Therefore, we utilized the Node-Level and Network-Level to measure the local and global aspects of any undirected social network.

Given an undirected social network on YouTube, $G = (V, E)$, where V in the network represents number of commenters, and E in the graph represents common videos between two commenters. Find the κ small influential sets of individuals that can maximize the influence in V. The focal structure sets in G are measured $F = \{G'\}$, where $G' = (V', E')$ and $V' \subseteq V$ and $E' \subseteq E$. For all i and j, $i \neq j$, $G_i \in F$ and $G_j \in F$, such that no two FSA groups can incorporate each other, or $G_i \subsetneq G_j$ and $G_j \subsetneq G_i$ [5]. Each focal structure should be small or at least contain a triangle of nodes and can connect friends or have high clustering coefficient values than the graph measured value ($AC_F > 0$). The number of focal structure sets are not known in prior, where it can be equal to or less than the total number of nodes $|F| \leq |V|$.

3.1   Data Set

The model implemented in this research was applied to many other social networks such as Zachary's karate network [5, 31], Les Miserable [32], Saudi Arabia woman activities network [5], and a YouTube channel posting conspiracy theory videos [4]. The dataset used in this paper is an undirected network of YouTube commenters commenting on a channel, having more than fifteen million views, spreading fake news related to the conflict in the South China Sea as shown in Fig. 2. The dataset had more than 47,265 comments coming from 8,477 commenters on 5,095 videos, and the obtained network had more than 1 million edges as shown below.

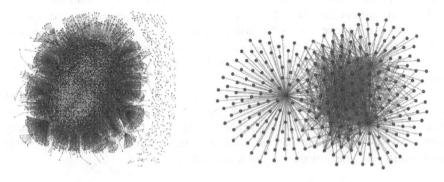

Fig. 2. YouTube commenter network (videos in green colors and commenters in Red color). The Right side shows the weigh ten commenters network clustered into different communities based on modularity method. (Color figure online)

3.2   Node-Level Sphere of Influence

Measuring the sphere of influence based on the number of links connected to a node would reveal information about the power, resources, and opportunities of that node in the network structure, as shown in Fig. 3. For this purpose, the degree centrality method is utilized to maximize the preferred nodes degree centrality values as shown in the model below (Eqs. 1–12). In this step, the model needs to measure all available nodes and exclude those that have only one neighbor. Considering all available nodes in the solution procedure helps overcome modularity's drawback of being unable to cluster small sets [33].

The second step in this section is related to the node's neighbors, where the model needs to consider the friendships between the neighbors [6]. For this purpose, the average clustering coefficient method is employed to evaluate the local groups' intra-connections, as shown in Fig. 4. The model would filter out any chain sets or groups that have low average clustering coefficient values.

$$max \sum_{i=1}^{n} \delta_i \tag{1}$$

Subject to

$$\delta_i = \{d\vec{c}_1 \preccurlyeq d\vec{c}_2 \preccurlyeq d\vec{c}_3 \preccurlyeq \cdots \preccurlyeq d\vec{c}_i\} - \overline{dc_j^Q} \quad \forall i,j \tag{2}$$

$$d_i^c = \sum_j m_{ij} \quad \forall i \tag{3}$$

$$d_i^c \geq 2 \quad \forall i \tag{4}$$

$$D_G^L = \frac{1}{n} \sum_{i=1}^{n} d_i^c \tag{5}$$

$$D_G^L < \hat{d}_i^c \leq D_G^U \quad \forall i \tag{6}$$

$$a_i^c = \frac{(\# \ of \ Triangles) \times 3}{\# \ of \ Connected \ Triples \ of \ Nodes} \quad \forall i,j,z \tag{7}$$

$$AC_G^L = \frac{1}{n} \sum_{i=1}^{n} a_i^c \tag{8}$$

$$AC_G^L < a_i^c \leq AC_G^U \quad \forall i \tag{9}$$

$$\overrightarrow{C_v} = \{\vec{c_1}, \vec{c_2}, \vec{c_3}, \ldots, \vec{c_i}\} - \overline{c_j^Q} \quad \forall i,j \tag{10}$$

$$\vec{c\delta_i} = \overrightarrow{C_{\delta_i}} \quad \forall i \tag{11}$$

$$F = \left\{ c_1, \overline{c_j^Q}, \overline{c_{j+1}^Q}, \ldots, \overline{c_\kappa^Q} \right\} \quad \forall j, \kappa \tag{12}$$

Where Eqs. (1), and (2), maximize the preferred degree centrality δ_i, $i = 1$ is the lowest central set and $i = n$ is the highest central set. Excluding any set imported from the Network-Level $\overline{dc_j^Q}$ that has maximized the graph modularity as shown in Fig. 5. Equation (3), is to measure the node's sphere of influence (d_i^c), m_{ij} is the number of j nodes connected to node i. Equation (4), all nodes must have more than one neighbor, otherwise, the they will be excluded from the solution procedure. Equation (5), measures the D_G^L, average degree centrality's lower bound and n is the number of nodes as shown in Fig. 3. Equation (6), is to filter the sets based on their normalized degree centrality, $\hat{d}_i^c$, and D_G^U is the upper bound which is equal to the highest calculated d^c in the network. Equation (7) measures the node friends' connectivity, if $a_i^c = 1$, then all the set's member are friends, considering it as upper bound (UB), otherwise if $a_i^c = 0$, then the group is a chain group and should be excluded from the solution procedure. Equation (8) measures the graph's average clustering coefficient value, where AC_G^L is the lower bound (LB). Equation (9) measures the local communities average clustering coefficient, a_i^c and the results should not violate both (UB, LB). In constraint (10), the ascending sorted set of vectors for the local communities are generated, excluding $\overline{c_j^Q}$, imported from the Network-Level. Equation (11), $\vec{c\delta_i}$ is a parameter to transfer the selected local community from Node-Level to the Network-Level. Equation (12) is the model output containing sets that maximized centrality and jointly maximized the graph modularity values. These are the focal structure sets candidates.

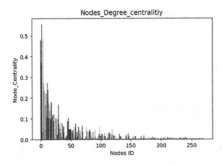

Fig. 3. Degree centrality measures.

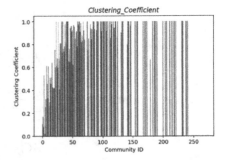

Fig. 4. Avg. clustering coefficient values.

3.3 Network-Level Analysis

Implementing the spectral modularity [34–36] will save lots of calculation complexity in the model. This section is designed to find a set of nodes that jointly would maximize the graph modularity, as shown in Fig. 5. The following set of equations describe the Network-Level procedure.

$$max \sum_{j=1}^{n} \varrho_j^M \tag{13}$$

Subject to

$$\varrho_j^M = \{\varrho_1, \varrho_2, \varrho_3, \ldots, \varrho_j\} \quad \forall j \tag{14}$$

$$\delta_j = \{\vec{c_1}, \vec{c_2}, \vec{c_3}, \ldots, \vec{c_n}\} - \overline{c\delta_i} \quad \forall j \tag{15}$$

$$B = A_{ij} - \frac{dd^T}{2m} \quad \forall i, j \tag{16}$$

$$\xi_j = \{\overline{c\delta_i} \cup \delta_j | \overline{\delta_i} \neq \delta_j\} \quad \forall j \tag{17}$$

$$\varrho_j = \frac{1}{2m} Tr\left(\xi_j B \xi_j^T\right) \quad \forall j \tag{18}$$

$$\varrho^l \leq \varrho_j \leq \varrho^U \quad \forall j \tag{19}$$

where Eqs. (13) and (14), are used to maximize the graph modularity values. Constraint (15), is the set of vectors candidates inherited from the Node-level excluding $\overline{c\delta_i}$, as shown in Fig. 5. Equation (16), is the graph modularity matrix, where $d \in R^{n \times 1}$, is the degree vector for all nodes, m is the number of nodes in the graph, and A_{ij}, is the graph adjacency matrix. Constraint (17), ξ_j is a union between the set imported from the Node-Level $\overline{c\delta_i}$ and the candidate community δ_j that presumably will join the subgraph as shown in Fig. 5. Equation (18) calculates the spectral modularity for any given graph that has $\xi_j \in R^{n \times k}, k = \{1, 2, \ldots, n\}$ partitions. Equation (19) used to make sure that the generated modularity values will not violate the modularity bounds $LB = \varrho^l$, and $UB = \varrho^U$.

In the next step, we utilized a multi-criteria problem to weight the identified focal structure sets based on small real-world network metrics as shown in Eq. (20), where ρ_{Fi} is the rank of any explored focal structure set. The aim of the implemented method is to assign a higher weight to those groups that maximized the degree centrality (ADC_F), average clustering coefficient (AC), and density values (DN) as shown in Eq. (22). Likewise, a higher weight is assigned to any set that minimized the diameter (R_D) and the average path length (R_{Al}) [6].

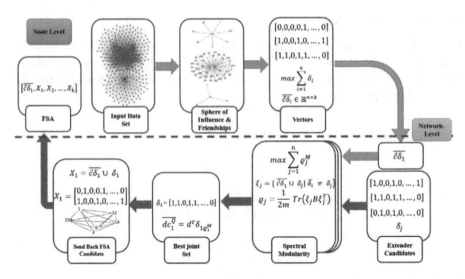

Fig. 5. Shows the interactions between Node-Level and Network-Level, where the assigned parameters are transferring vectors from the Node-Level to the Network-Level. likewise, the Network-level will transfer the best set of nodes that jointly maximized the modularity value.

The following sets of equations is to rank all explored focal structure sets. W_{Fi}, is the weight of a metric when it is close to its max/ min respectively and x is the actual value of each metric. The numeric thresholds are tunable and can be assigned by the user.

$$\rho_{Fi} = \frac{1}{5}(R_{AC} + R_{ADC} + R_{DN} + R_D + R_{Al}) \tag{20}$$

$$R_{AC} = \begin{cases} W_{Fi} = 5 & \mathcal{AC}_{Fi} \geq x \\ W_{Fi} = 4 & x > \mathcal{AC}_{Fi} \geq 0.9x \\ W_{Fi} = 3 & 0.9x > \mathcal{AC}_{Fi} \geq 0.8x \\ W_{Fi} = 2 & 0.8x > \mathcal{AC}_{Fi} \geq 0.6x \\ W_{Fi} = 1 & otherwise \end{cases} \tag{21}$$

$$R_{Al} = \begin{cases} W_{Fi} = 5 & \mathcal{Al}_{Fi} \leq y \\ W_{Fi} = 4 & y < \mathcal{Al}_{Fi} \leq 1.5y \\ W_{Fi} = 3 & 1.5y < \mathcal{Al}_{Fi} \leq 2y \\ W_{Fi} = 2 & 2y < \mathcal{Al}_{Fi} \leq 3y \\ W_{Fi} = 1 & otherwise \end{cases} \tag{22}$$

The results after applying the above multi-criteria model to the identified focal structure sets, prove that most of the prioritized sets have high rank scores, see Fig. 8.

4 Experimental Results

In this part of the paper, we monitor the small influential sets of commenters hidden inside a big channel spreading the fake news. This commenter network was constructed by connecting two commenters if they commented on the same video. The model identified twenty-nine focal structure sets, the majority of them atomic sets as shown in Figs. 7 and 12. These groups did not violate the evaluation metrics applied in the previous section. Figure 6 shows the identified focal structure sets and their belonging commenters. The structures of the identified sets proved that all focal structure sets have influential commenters appear in different groups.

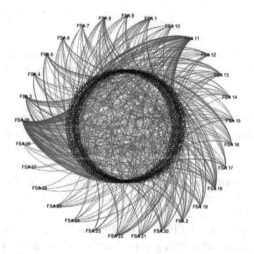

Fig. 6. Focal structure sets explored from the YouTube dataset.

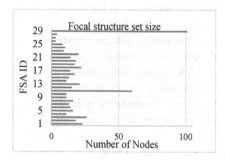

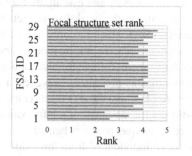

Fig. 7. Identified focal structure sets size.

Fig. 8. Most of the focal structure sets have high rank.

These groups have enough resources to spread information to most parts of the network, as shown in Fig. 9, where all identified sets have high degree centrality values compared to the graph's value.

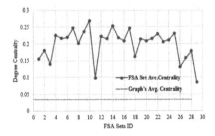

Fig. 9. Average degree centrality of focal structure sets vs. graph value.

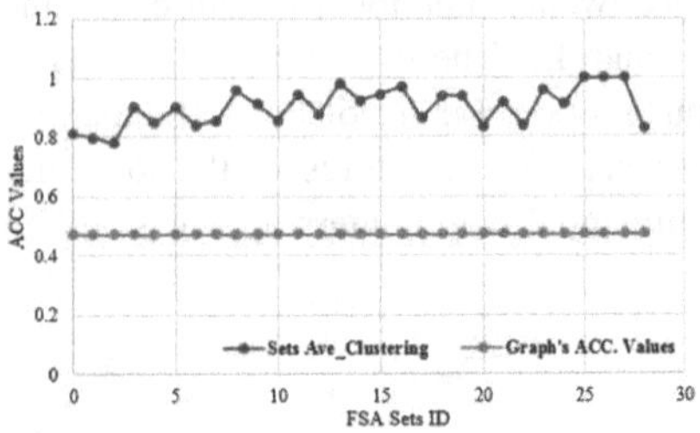

Fig. 10. Average Clustering Coefficient (ACC) of focal structure sets, vs. graph.

Since the identified focal structure sets are central and denser than regular communities, their intra coordination gives them enough power and resources for spreading fake news to other users, deceive the crowds in the network, and control the network's mood as shown in Fig. 10.

Next, we would demonstrate experimentally the significance of these focal structure sets by removing them from the network and measuring their impact on network's connectivity and information diffusion. Figure 11 shows the disruption in the network's connectivity generated by FSA 1, 11, 13, and 22. (Due to space limitation, we do not show the impact of other FSA groups, but similar disruption was observed). The left side shows small influential set of individuals that could maximize the information diffusion in the network. These identified FSA groups are central to the network, have higher connectivity and essentially control the flow of information in the network. The right side shows the focal structure sets impact on other individuals in the network. For example, FSA1 which has only twenty-three nodes, has access to the entire network, it can send and receive information to and from three major communities identified by modularity method (orange, blue, and red). Also, FSA 11, has high influence on two communities as presented. However, a higher impact can be observed from FSA 13, and FSA 22, where these two sets consisted of individuals that make them the strongest candidates for the network's information diffusion. As shown in the figure, they have gained a unique position helped them to control the information flow for a huge number of individuals' from three different major communities. These small sets have the ability to influence the top number of individuals.

The significance of the identified hidden sets is related to their impact in the network, where, they are small size sets, including central nodes acting in different communities, and they did not behave like regular communities.

The implemented algorithm identified higher number of intensive communities than the modularity method, where the latter method only identified 6 major communities and could not identify sets explored by our method as shown in Appendix A. Also, the modularity method failed to identify a very important structure, i.e., #29 shown in Fig. 12 (left side). This set includes central nodes from several communities that make it the power center in the network.

The other identified influential sets presented in Appendix A can generate huge disruption in the network's connectivity, spread huge amount of information, and can access to the most part of the network. Their structures allow them higher power than a single influential node and more interaction than a regular community.

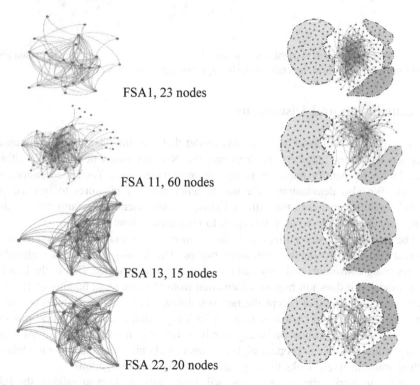

FSA1, 23 nodes

FSA 11, 60 nodes

FSA 13, 15 nodes

FSA 22, 20 nodes

Fig. 11. Demonstrating the influence of key sets or focal structures of commenters for a YouTube channel.

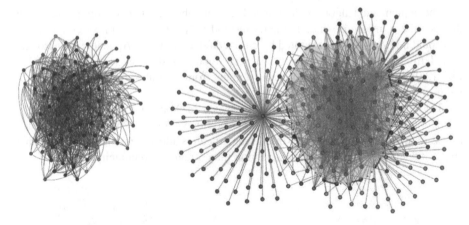

Fig. 12. Modularity method (right side) did not identify structure 29, one of the significant FSA sets identified by the focal structure analysis implemented in this paper

5   Conclusion and Discussion

In this paper, we explained our max-max model that uses the Node-based community detection algorithm (degree centrality) and the Network-based detection algorithms (modularity) to identify intensive groups of commenters in a YouTube commenters network. We also demonstrated the use of other network measures to increase the results' resolution and rank the extracted groups. These identified groups were central to the network and served as gatekeepers to information flow.

The proposed model utilizes a decomposition and a multi-criteria optimization procedure to identify the key intensive groups, but it also validates the identified clusters using constraints and only valid focal structure set selected. One of the benefits of the model is it does not require information from the user (e.g., number of clusters, lower and upper bounds) except the network dataset. Finally, the model was able to overcome drawbacks of current state of art FSA algorithm and finds smallest possible sets as key intensive groups including members that span multiple FSA groups. Also, this algorithm was able to propose higher number of atomic groups than the modularity method and effectively ranks these groups for in-depth investigations.

For future works, the research team will invest lots of effort to validate the FSA analysis results. Network's resiliency should be measured within the analysis. Betweenness centrality needs consideration and optimizing the solution procedure by comparing all available methods.

Acknowledgment. This research is funded in part by the U.S. National Science Foundation (IIS-1636933, ACI-1429160, and IIS-1110868), U.S. Office of Naval Research (N00014-10-1-0091, N00014-14-1-0489, N00014-15-P-1187, N00014-16-1- 2016, N00014-16-1-2412, N00014-17-1-2605, N00014-17- 1-2675, N00014-19-1-2336), U.S. Air Force Research Lab, U. S. Army Research Office (W911NF-16-1-0189), U.S. Defense Advanced Research Projects Agency (W31P4Q-17-C-0059), Arkansas Research Alliance, and the Jerry L. Maulden/Entergy

Foundation at the University of Arkansas–Little Rock. Any opinions, findings, and conclusions or recommendations expressed in this material are those of the authors and do not necessarily reflect the views of the funding organizations.

References

1. Leskovec, J., Kleinberg, J., Faloutsos, C.: Graphs over time: densification laws, shrinking diameters and possible explanations. In: Proceedings of Eleventh ACM SIGKDD International Conference on Knowledge Discovery in Data Mining, pp. 177–187 (2005)
2. Sato, K., Izunaga, Y.: An enhanced MILP-based branch-and-price approach to modularity density maximization on graphs. Comput. Oper. Res. **106**, 1–25 (2018)
3. Von Luxburg, U.: A tutorial on spectral clustering. Stat. Comput. **17**(4), 395–416 (2007)
4. Alassad, M., Agarwal, N., Hussain, M.N.: Examining intensive groups in YouTube commenter networks. In: Thomson, R., Bisgin, H., Dancy, C., Hyder, A. (eds.) Social, Cultural, and Behavioral Modeling. SBP-BRiMS 2019. LNCS, vol. 11549, pp. 224–233. Springer, Cham (2019). https://doi.org/10.1007/978-3-030-21741-9_23
5. Şen, F., Wigand, R., Agarwal, N., Tokdemir, S., Kasprzyk, R.: Focal structures analysis: identifying influential sets of individuals in a social network. Soc. Netw. Anal. Min. **6**(1), 17 (2016)
6. Zafarani, R., Abbasi, M.A., Liu, H.: Social Media Mining: An Introduction. Cambridge University Press, Cambridge (2014)
7. Hussain, M.N., Tokdemir, S., Agarwal, N., Al-Khateeb, S.: Analyzing disinformation and crowd manipulation tactics on YouTube. In: 2018 IEEE/ACM International Conference on Advances in Social Networks Analysis and Mining, pp. 1092–1095 (2018)
8. Page, L., Brin, S., Motwani, R., Winograd, T.: The PageRank citation ranking: bringing order to the web. World Wide Web Internet Web Inf. Syst. **54**(1999–66), 1–17 (1998)
9. Kleinberg, J.O.N.M.: Authoritative sources in a hyperlinked environment. In: Proceedings of the ACM-SIAM Symposium on Discrete Algorithms, vol. 46, no. 5, pp. 604–632 (1999)
10. Herzig, J., Mass, Y., Roitman, H.: An author-reader influence model for detecting topic-based influencers in social media. In: Proc. 25th ACM Conference on Hypertext and Social Media, pp. 46–55 (2014)
11. Yang, L., Silva, J.C., Papageorgiou, L.G., Tsoka, S.: Community structure detection for directed networks through modularity optimisation. Algorithms **9**(4), 1–10 (2016)
12. Briscoe, E.J., Appling, D.S., Mappus, R.L., Hayes, H.: Determining credibility from social network structure. In: Proceedings of 2013 IEEE/ACM International Conference on Advances in Social Networks Analysis and Mining, pp. 1418–1424 (2014)
13. Jones, S., O'Neill, E.: Feasibility of structural network clustering for group-based privacy control in social networks. In: proceedings of the Sixth Symposium on Usable Privacy and Security, p. 9 (2010)
14. Leskovec, J., McGlohon, M., Faloutsos, C., Glance, N., Hurst, M.: Cascading behavior in large blog graphs. In: Proceedings of the 2007 SIAM International Conference on Data Mining, pp. 551–556 (2007)
15. Li, C., Wang, L., Sun, S., Xia, C.: Identification of influential spreaders based on classified neighbors in real-world complex networks. Appl. Math. Comput. **320**(11), 512–523 (2018)
16. Borgatti, S.P.: Centrality and network flow. Soc. Networks **27**(1), 55–71 (2005)
17. Agarwal, N., Liu, H., Tang, L., Yu, P.S.: Modeling blogger influence in a community. Soc. Netw. Anal. Min. **2**(2), 139–162 (2012)

18. Richardson, M., Domingos, P.: Mining knowledge-sharing sites for viral marketing. In: Proceedings of eighth ACM SIGKDD International Conference on Knowledge Discovery and Data Mining, pp. 61–70 (2002)
19. Kempe, D., Kleinberg, J.: Maximizing the spread of influence through a social network. In: Proceedings of ninth ACM SIGKDD International Conference on Knowledge Discovery and Data Mining, pp. 137–146 (2003)
20. Chen, W., Wang, Y.: Efficient influence maximization in social networks categories and subject descriptors. In: Proceedings of 15th ACM SIGKDD International Conference on Knowledge Discovery and Data Mining, pp. 199–207 (2009)
21. Leskovec, J., Mcglohon, M., Faloutsos, C., Glance, N., Hurst, M.: Patterns of cascading behavior in large blog graphs. In: Proceedings of 2007 SIAM International Conference on Data Mining, pp. 551–556 (2007)
22. Newman, M.E.J.: Modularity and community structure in networks. Proc. Natl. Acad. Sci. **103**(23), 8577–8582 (2006)
23. Girvan, M., Newman, M.: Community structure in social and biological networks. PNAS **99**(12), 7821–7826 (2002)
24. Sato, K., Izunaga, Y.: A branch-and-price approach with MILP formulation to modularity density maximization on graphs, pp. 1–25 (2017)
25. Chan, E.Y.K., Yeung, D.Y.: A convex formulation of modularity maximization for community detection. In: IJCAI International Joint Conference on Artificial Intelligence, pp. 2218–2225 (2011)
26. Izunaga, Y., Yamamoto, Y.: A cutting plane algorithm with heuristics for separation problem, no. 1309, pp. 1–12 (2013)
27. Kehagias, A., Pitsoulis, L.: Bad communities with high modularity. Eur. Phys. J. B **86**(7), 330 (2013)
28. Dinh, T.N., Thai, M.T.: Community detection in scale-free networks: approximation algorithms for maximizing modularity. IEEE J. Sel. Areas Commun. **31**(6), 997–1006 (2013)
29. de Santiago, R., Lamb, L.C.: Exact computational solution of modularity density maximization by effective column generation. Comput. Oper. Res. **86**, 18–29 (2017)
30. Reichardt, J., Bornholdt, S.: When are networks truly modular? Phys. D Nonlinear Phenom. **224**(1–2), 20–26 (2006)
31. Zachary, W.W.: An information flow model for conflict and fission in small groups. J. Anthropol. Res. **33**(4), 452–473 (1977)
32. Hugo, V.: Les misérables. TY Crowell & Company (1887)
33. Tsung, C.K., Ho, H., Chou, S., Lin, J., Lee, S.: A spectral clustering approach based on modularity maximization for community detection problem. In: Proceedings of 2016 International Computer Symposium, ICS 2016, pp. 12–17 (2017)
34. Newman, M.E.J.: Detecting community structure in networks. Eur. Phys. J. B - Condens. Matter **38**(2), 321–330 (2004)
35. Newman, M.E.J.: Fast algorithm for detecting community structure in networks. Rev. E Stat. Phys. Plasmas Fluids Relat. Interdiscip. Top. **69**(6), 5 (2004)
36. Girvan, M., Newman, M.E.J.: Community structure in social and biological networks. Proc. Natl. Acad. Sci. **99**(12), 7821–7826 (2002)

An International Comparative Analysis for Autonomous Vehicles and Their Effects

Ryosuke Ando[1]([⊠]) [ID], Wei Liu[2], Jia Yang[1], and Yasuhide Nishihori[1]

[1] TTRI (Toyota Transportation Research Institute), Toyota 471-0024, Japan
ando@ttri.or.jp
[2] Chongqing Jiaotong University, Chongqing, China

Abstract. Recently, autonomous vehicles have been one of the hottest issues in the world. In the pasted century, automobile vehicles have changed human lives and social society. From now, autonomous vehicles will change the world for the second time. Therefore, the issue of autonomous vehicles calls us to focus its effects on the related social respects. In order to investigate the effects of these innovative technologies, an international comparative study between Japan and China, No. 2 and No. 3 largest economic countries in the world, were conducted during 2016 and 2018, respectively. In this paper, we report on the results of two questionnaire surveys. Through this comparative study, we can understand the similarity and difference between these two countries and reconsider what we should do in the coming years. The major findings indicated that the Japanese are more conservative than the Chinese. In terms of the comparative results, we proposed that it was crucial for Japanese society to change this situation to promote autonomous vehicles.

Keywords: Autonomous vehicles · Innovative technology ·
International comparison · Japan · China

1 Introduction

Autonomous vehicles have been one of the hottest issues in the world. In the pasted century, automobile vehicles have changed human lives and social society. From now, autonomous vehicles will change the world for the second time. Therefore, the issue of autonomous vehicles calls us to focus its effects on the related social respects.

Regarding international comparison on autonomous vehicles, these has been some studies such as (References [3, 4, 6, 7, 12]) by the researchers in Japan and other countries. However, the study targeted on China is very limited since Chinese government set forth a very strict limitation on the personal information. Therefore, in this paper, we report on the results of two questionnaire surveys implemented in China and Japan (Reference [1]), respectively. They are ranked as the second and third economic countries worldwide. Through the comparative analysis, we can understand the similarity and difference between them, and reconsider what we should do in the coming years.

The methodologies to discuss competences and its uncertainty of science and technology have been made in many existed studies (References [2, 5, 8–11]) by

© Springer Nature Switzerland AG 2019
N. Agarwal et al. (Eds.): MSBC 2019, CCIS 1079, pp. 55–67, 2019.
https://doi.org/10.1007/978-3-030-29862-3_5

Ayse Ozmen, Gerhard-Wilhelm Weber, Pakize Taylan, Silja Meyer-Nieberg and Erik
Kropat et al. What we are reporting in this paper is not the deep methodology but the
useful information for further analysis.

2   Outline of the Surveys

An internet-based survey in Japan was conducted in October 2016 through Rakuten
Research. This corporation (currently renamed as Rakuten Insight) is one of the largest
websites for market research in Japan. There were 2,200,000 registered monitors. 1,480
respondents owning and driving cars were randomly selected to answer our survey.

On the other hand, the survey in China was conducted during December 2017 and
January 2018. Considering the people in China are more likely to use SNS such as
Weibo and WeChat. So both Weibo and WeChat were used with the website together.
1,500 respondents driving cars took part in this survey.

The question sheets have been treated almost the same in both Japan and China.
However, a few of contents, such as annual income and year of using cars, had been
adjusted by considering the different present states and the difference of survey
implementation.

The basic statistic approaches used here are F-test as shown in Eq. (1) and t-test as
shown in Eq. (2).

$$F = S_1^2/S_2^2 \tag{1}$$

where S_i^2 is the variance of sample i (i means Japan or China).

$$t = d/(\sqrt{s_d^2/n}) \tag{2}$$

where d is the difference and n is the sample number.

The result of purchased cars is using as shown in Fig. 1, almost 50% of respondents
in Japan purchased in the past three years and more than 10% of people purchased 10
years before. In China, more than 80% of people purchased in the past five years and
only 33% of respondents purchased cars in 2005 or before.

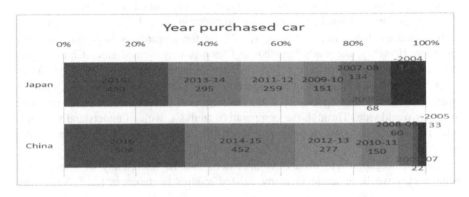

Fig. 1. When did you purchase your car?

As given in Fig. 2, the household incomes in China are generally lower than that in Japan. Furthermore, the percentages of the relatively low-income class are larger than that in Japan. The household income distributes more evenly in Japan, compared to China.

Household classification makes the car using different. Figure 3 shows us that "couple only" families and "two generations with children" families in Japan shows more than that in China. Comparatively, "single" and "three generations with parent" families in China show larger shares than that in Japan. The F-value is 4.284 and greater than 4.28 (with the degrees of freedom as 6 for both Japan sample and China sample).

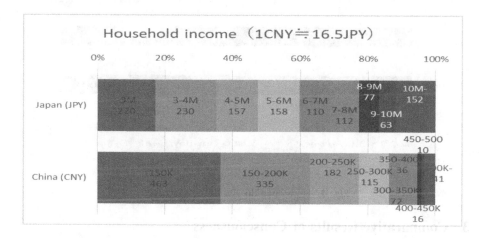

(where M=million, K=thousand, CNY=Chinese yuan, JPY=Japanese yen)

Fig. 2. How much is your household annual income?

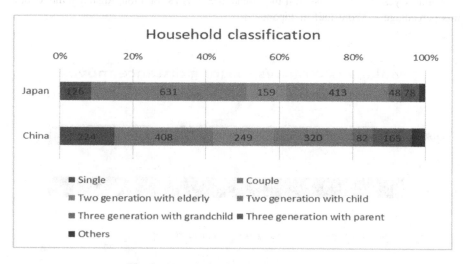

Fig. 3. Household classification comparison

In daily life, Japanese people make use of cars more frequently than Chinese people as Fig. 4. Nearly 20% of Chinese people drive their cars for less than one day per month. This may be because owing cars is not only for mobility needs but also for showing the economic status of the car owner. The F-value is 5.0503 and greater than 5.05 (with the degrees of freedom as 5 for both Japan sample and China sample).

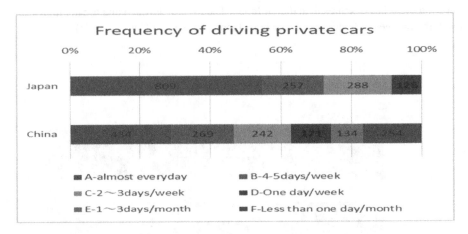

Fig. 4. How often do you drive your cars?

3   Comparative Results of Consciousness

At first, some questions on how people want to make use the autonomous vehicles (AVs) are compared and shown from Figs. 5, 6, 7, 8, 9, 10 and 11.

We can know from Fig. 5 that more than 40% of people in China answered that "absolutely yes" when we asked if they make use of AVs for a long-distance move, but this percentage is about half in Japan.

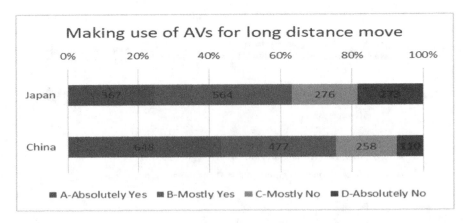

Fig. 5. Do you want to make use of AVs for a long-distance move? (p-value = 0.975)

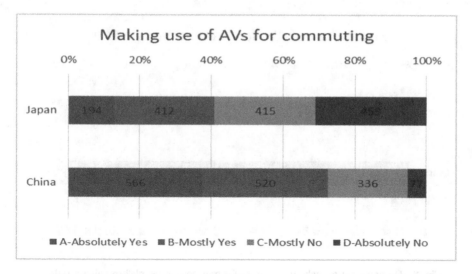

Fig. 6. Do you want to make use of AVs for commuting? (p-value = 0.978)

Regarding whether people make use of AVs for commuting, in both China and Japan, as depicted in Fig. 6, the percentages of "absolutely yes" have been decreased. However, the difference between the two countries became larger. That in Japan is less than half of that in China.

As for the daily life activities such as shopping, seeing doctors and amusement activities, the situations shown in Fig. 7 in both countries are almost the same as what in Fig. 6. Furthermore, on transporting people given in Fig. 8, quite similar results can be obtained.

Meanwhile, given by Fig. 9, about access transport which means that short trips as the first one mile or the last one mile, the percentages of both "absolutely yes" and "mostly yes" decrease in both countries although there are still more than 50% of people answered positively in China.

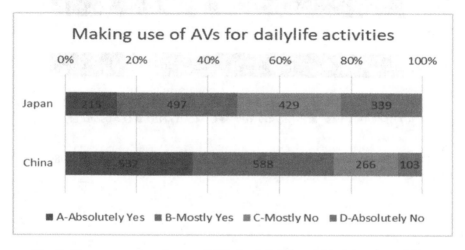

Fig. 7. Do you want to make use of AVs for daily life activities? (p-value = 0.987)

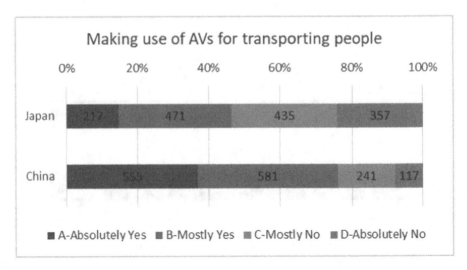

Fig. 8. Do you want to make use of AVs for transporting people? (p-value = 0.981)

In China, people gave the highest expecting business activities (almost 80% answered "yes" as shown in Fig. 10) and automated parking (80% answered "yes" as Fig. 11 shows). However, in Japan, people told us quite different results on these two questions: higher expecting for automated parking but lower expecting for business activities.

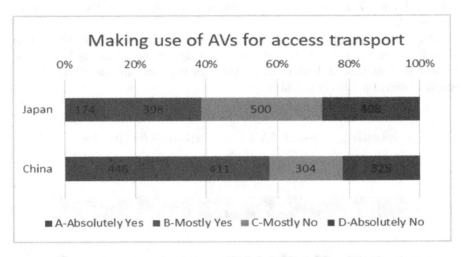

Fig. 9. Do you want to make use of AVs for access transport? (p-value = 0.989)

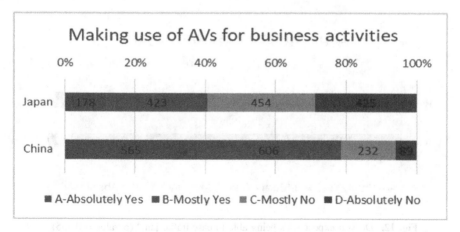

Fig. 10. Do you want to make use of AVs for business activities? (p-value = 0.988)

Making a short summary, we can know that Chinese people higher expected AVs for all usage situation than Japanese people.

Traffic jam, traffic accidents, and traffic environmental issues are normally considered as three negative outputs that automobile vehicles have brought into our society. In our surveys, we set some questions to understand people's expecting for AVs to solve or contribute these three negative outputs.

The questions are summarized in Figs. 12, 13 and 14. Both Chinese people and Japanese people have a higher expectation that AVs will solve/contribute to the three negative outputs. Of these three issues, to reduce traffic accidents is the most expected in both countries: more than 80% are expecting. Furthermore, the distributions are also very similar, that made t-test be with a low p-value (0.875 < 0.9). Regarding the traffic jam and environmental issues, the results are similar, too although the distributions are statistically different. Moreover, what expected by Chinese people are higher than what by Japanese people.

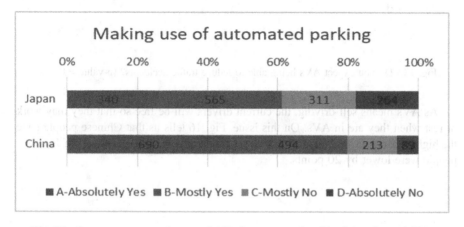

Fig. 11. Do you want to make use of AVs for automated parking? (p-value = 0.991)

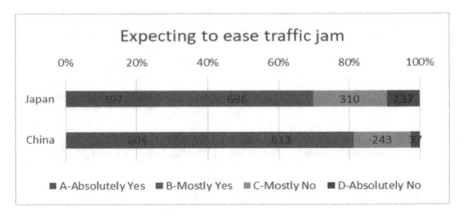

Fig. 12. Do you expect AVs being able to ease traffic jam? (p-value = 0.955)

In Japan, the aging issue has been a very serious social issue. On the other hand, China's aging increases very quickly and will be No. 1 in the near future. Therefore, the contribution of AVs to support elderly's transport has been higher expected in both countries (Fig. 15). In Japan, this issue is the highest expected issue.

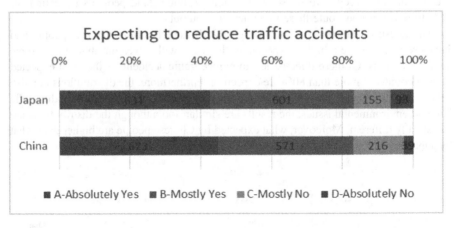

Fig. 13. Do you expect AVs being able to reduce traffic accidents? (p-value = 0.875)

As AVs means self-driving, the current drivers will be free so that they may work or rest when they are in AVs. On this issue, Fig. 16 tells us that Chinese people gave the highest percentage of positive answers. Comparatively, the percentages of Japanese people were lower by 20 points.

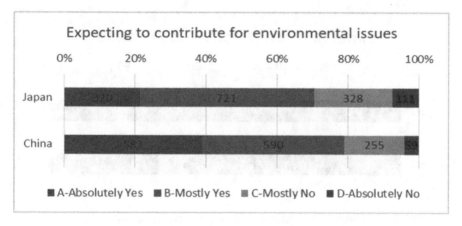

Fig. 14. Do you expect AVs being able to contribute to environmental issues? (p-value = 0.988)

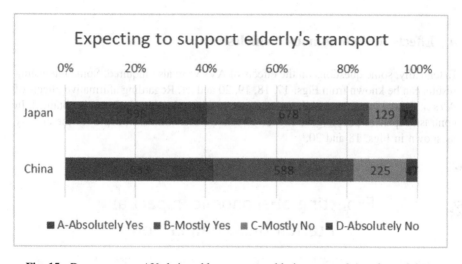

Fig. 15. Do you expect AVs being able to support elder's transport? (p-value = 0.940)

Summarizing the above, we can know that Chinese people have almost the same percentage to make use of AVs and expect AVs positively contributing to the solution of the automobile traffic problems and the related social issues. On the other hand, Japanese people show the higher expecting for AVs to contribute to the solution of the automobile traffic problems and the related social issues, but the percentages of making use of AVs are quite lower. Japanese people seemed not being imaging themselves in the coming AVs society.

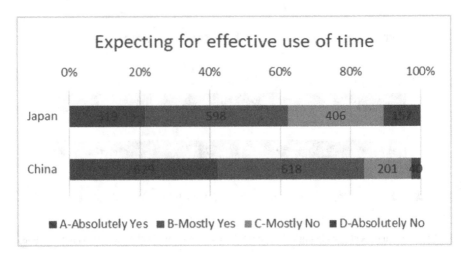

Fig. 16. Do you expect AVs being able to contribute for effective use of time? (p-value = 0.987)

4 Effects of Autonomous Vehicles

Extendedly, some questions on the effects of AVs were also inquired. Some interesting results can be known from Figs. 17, 18, 19, 20 and 21. Regarding affirmative effects of AVs in Figs. 17 and 21, a higher percentage in China than that in Japan is obtained. In contrast, Japanese people gave higher percentage than Chinese people for the anxiety as shown in Figs. 18 and 20.

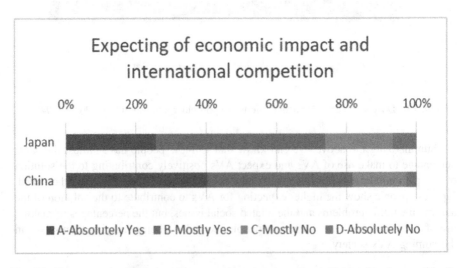

Fig. 17. Do you expect AVs being able to contribute to economics and international competition? (p-value = 0.985)

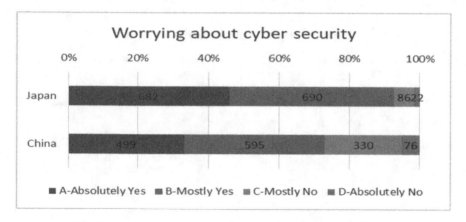

Fig. 18. Do you worry AVs about cybersecurity? (p-value = 0.961)

Extremely, on "worrying about cybersecurity" and "worrying about responsibilities of traffic accidents", more than 90% of Japanese people answered "yes". How to let Japanese people get rid of their anxiety on AVs seems to be an important task for the people to promote the AVs.

More than 70% of Japanese people and more than 80% of Chinese people expect the economic impact of AVs (Fig. 17) and thought AVs contribute to international competition of their countries.

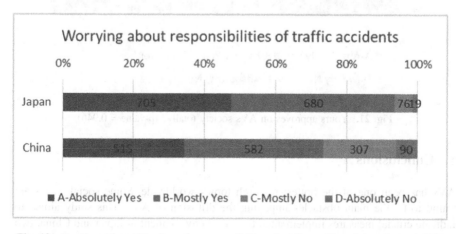

Fig. 19. Do you worry AVs about the responsibility of traffic accidents? (p-value = 0.972)

These also brought that more than 50% of people in both countries (Fig. 21) approve on AVs society totally. These results are a strong power to promote AVs into the real society in both two countries.

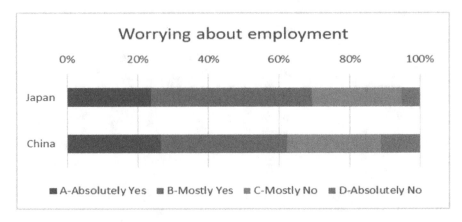

Fig. 20. Do you worry AVs about employment? (p-value = 0.960)

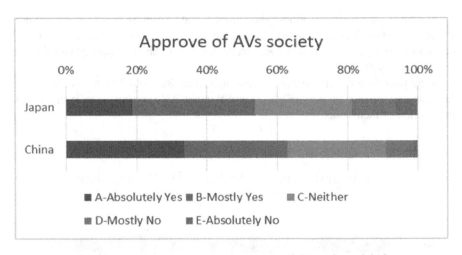

Fig. 21. Yours approves on AVs society totally? (p-value = 0.946)

5 Conclusions

AVs has been one of the hottest research topics worldwide. Some social issues are found to be the main obstacles impeding the diffusion of AVs. This study aimed to indicate crucial measures implemented for social environment in Japan and China, two top leader countries in the world, to welcome future society with AVs. To realize this goal, we have conducted an international comparative study between Japan and China. Here, the present state in China was investigated in 2018 based on the previous study in Japan in 2017.

The comparative results told us that Chinese people are more positive to affirm the AVs generally than Japanese people. Japanese people are more prudent when promoting AVs into real society. Although all people in both countries show the same result on expecting to reduce the traffic accidents by AVs and to contribute to support the elderly people's mobility, most results are in contrast.

When we are positive to rethink these results, the solutions in these two countries can tell the world how to overcome all kinds of obstacles in the process of promoting the AVs.

Acknowledgment. This study was partly supported by JSPS KAKENHI Grant Number JP17K06612.

References

1. Ando, R., Liu, W., Yang, J., Nishihori, Y.: A comparative analysis of people's consciousness on autonomous vehicles, traffic and transportation issues between Japan and China. In: Proceedings of Infrastructure Planning, vol. 58, pp. 1–5. JSCE, Tokyo (2018)
2. Ozmen, A., Kropat, E., Weber, G.-W.: Spline regression models for complex multi-modal regulatory network. Optim. Methods Softw. **29**(3), 515–534 (2014)
3. The Boston Consulting Group: Self-Driving Vehicles, Robo-Taxis, and the Urban Mobility Revolution (2016)
4. Schoettle, B., Sivak, M.: A survey of public opinion about autonomous and self-driving vehicles in the U.S., the U.K., and Australia. The report of the University of Michigan Transportation Research Institute (2014)
5. Weber, G.-W., Ozmen, A., Fraczyk-Kucharska, M., et al.: Knowledge acceleration by competences and multivariate adaptive regression splines. Presented at International Days of Competence for the future, Poznan (2018)
6. Knig, M., Neumayr, L.: Users' resistance towards radical innovations: the case of the self-driving car. Transp. Res. Part F: Traffic Psychol. Behav. **44**, 42–52 (2017)
7. Ministry of Internal Affairs and Communications, Japan: WHITE PAPER 2016 Information and Communications in Japan (2016)
8. Taylan, P., Weber, G.-W.: A classification model based on multivariate adaptive regression splines (MARS). In: Societal Complexity, Data Mining and Gaming – State-of-the-Art 2017. Greenhill & Waterfront, Amsterdam/Guilford/Montreal (2017)
9. Taylan, P., Weber, G.-W., et al.: Continuous optimization applied in MARS for modern applications in finance, science and technology. Presented at IFORS 2008, Sandton (2008)
10. Meyer-Nieberg, S., Kropat, E.: Can evolution strategies benefit from shrinkage estimators? Trans. Comput. Collect. Intell. **28**, 116–142 (2018)
11. Meyer-Nieberg, S., Kropat, E.: Evolution strategies and covariance matrix adaptation – investigating new shrinkage techniques. In: ICAART, no. 2, pp. 105-116 (2016)
12. Wang, Z., Taniguchi, A., Enoch, M., Ieromonachou, P., Morikawa, T.: Social acceptance of autonomous vehicles – comparative analysis of Japan and UK. In: Proceedings of Infrastructure Planning, vol. 58, pp. 1–5. JSCE, Tokyo (2018)

An Investigation of Social-Behavioral Phenomena in the Peer-Review Processes of Scientific Foundations

George Kleiner[1,2]([✉]) [ID], Maxim Rybachuk[1,2]([✉]) [ID],
and Dmitry Ushakov[3]

[1] Central Economics and Mathematics Institute of the Russian Academy
of Sciences, 47 Nakhimovsky Ave., 117418 Moscow, Russia
george.kleiner@inbox.ru, m.ribachuk@gmail.com
[2] Financial University Under the Government of the Russian Federation,
49 Leningradsky Ave., 125993 Moscow, Russia
[3] Institute of Psychology of the Russian Academy of Sciences,
13b1 Yaroslavskaya Str., 129366 Moscow, Russia

Abstract. A huge amount of the issues in the realm of scientific endeavor are decided by member of expert communities in various fields. Decisions that sanction the funding of project proposals are based on a voting process. Such decision-making is particularly applied in the evaluation of applications to publicly-funded initiatives, which include the awarding of higher academic degrees and titles, in competitions to fill personnel vacancies, and other similar areas.

In such situations, experts (electors) individually decide in favor of a particular applicant based on specific objective criteria, as well by subjective consideration of their decision's repercussion in the profession field and the impact of the decisions on the experts' reputation. The result of such choices may depend on the psychological qualities and the current mood of the expert. The selection of the experts and their assignation to particular evaluation projects is often random. As a result, the collective adjudication on such projects is comprised of the interweaving of several objective and subjective factors.

In this paper, the authors examine the competitive selection process for scientific projects in applications for funding from scientific foundations. A simulated "peer review" model is utilized, designed to analyze a number of experts' economic and psychological characteristics and their group affiliation in the form of scientific schools.

The authors use qualitative analysis concerning the impact of changes reputations of experts on their decisions in the scientific community. Thus, the research results herein show the dynamics of the scientific and expert community structure. The model is agent-oriented and is a convenient tool for modeling the process of competitive selection in project funding applications.

Keywords: Public choice · Alternative choice · Science experts ·
Psychological characteristics · Agent-oriented modeling · Multi-stage choice ·
Reputation · Scientific school

© Springer Nature Switzerland AG 2019
N. Agarwal et al. (Eds.): MSBC 2019, CCIS 1079, pp. 68–81, 2019.
https://doi.org/10.1007/978-3-030-29862-3_6

1 Introduction

In developed countries, scientific endeavors are primarily supported by expenditure in the business sector. When arranged by country, the share of the total amount of funding in 2016 accounted for by such expenses was 78% in Japan, 74.7% in China, 65.6% in Germany, and 64.2% in the USA [1]. Conversely, funding in research, development and elaboration projects in Russia is accounted for mainly by state investment and in 2016 accounted for 68.2%, of such expenses. By comparison, the share of science funding in that year by the entrepreneurial sector amounted to 28.1%. Irrespective of these figures, the principal mechanism to support critical research initiative projects in Russia comes mainly from competitive funding efforts by way of scientific foundations [2, 3].

One should note the dissimilarity between the kinds of fundamental research which is funded by grants from scientific foundations, and the practical orientation research that is supported by other sources, e.g., state investment programs. As a rule, prospective fundamental research is motivated by natural ingenuity and the progress of material developments in a field and, in this way, provides an incentive towards the expansion of scientific knowledge. In 2016 in Russia the share of grants from foundations that support scientific, technical and innovative research accounted for only 2.4% [1]. By contrast, in the USA the same sector share is about 4%[1]. It is evident that in Russia the foundations grants share should be significantly increased in the coming years. This relates to the significant enhancement in scientific funds regulations and activities, as well as the improvement in the general mechanisms for competitive project selection [5].

Nowadays, in scientific foundations, in order to make decisions concerning the allocation of fundamental research support funds, multiple models of professional expertise are used. Various models can be utilised in several separate competitions within the same foundation. In this regard, one of the essential tasks of a scientific foundation is to choose and organize the best form of projects selection relative to the competitive financing system used. One of the most common approaches to solving this problem is an anonymous public review (*peer review*) carried out by scientists in expert roles in that particular field of science [6–9]. As a rule, the review is carried out via an electronic system by several independent experts who are selected for the review procedure at random. An alternative process is to adjudicate on each individual project success or failure by means of an expert council – a collegial group permanently composed of reputable scientists. In this case, if the identities and other information about the scientists involved in the peer-review process is hidden, the information about the expert council members is open and publicly available.

The chosen approaches are single-stage procedures, however, in reality, mixed (hybrid) multi-stage combinations of methods are used. Hybrid multi-stage methods are necessary for the purpose of increasing and varying the representation and independence of scientific project evaluations. For example, the final decision concerning project support can be made by the expert council based on the anonymous peer review

---

[1] The indicator reflects the share of the National Science Foundation to the overall expenditure on Science in the United States [4].

results. In this case, experts can be assigned ranks that reflect their qualifications. It should be noted that regardless of the evaluation methods and models used in scientific foundations, the examination of projects is carried out by qualified members of the scientific community. The main actors are scientists, and based on their set of opinions, the ultimate decisions concerning funding support or refusal is formed. Such scientific foundation entities, in turn, provide a platform for scientists to organize expert evaluation processes and carry out the distribution of funds, and act as an agent between the state and the scientific community (who may collectively be considered to represent 'science' as a field of endeavor).

Questions regarding the development of scientific foundation entities and the identification of appropriate independent research expertise have been raised repeatedly in the economic literature [10–13]. Several researchers have also pointed out the shortcomings of the examination methods used in the research projects, in particular those applied in the widely used anonymous public review method [14–19]. These authors have emphasized that one of the reasons for criticism of this method is its failure to take into account the individual economic and psychological characteristics of the adjudicating scientists. For an analysis of this hypothesis, the authors of this composition propose to use agent-based modeling tools [20, 21]. Such tools allow for a flexible approach to the construction of dynamic models of socio-economic systems functioning as a result of an individual economic agent's behavior. Examples of other classes of simulation models where we can see the impact of a participant's psychological characteristics on project result are presented in [22].

In a research project funded by the Russian Science Foundation (project No. 17-78-30035), the authors built an agent-oriented model of professional expertise and decision-making focusing on the support of scientific research projects, which takes into account economic and psychological characteristics of participants of this process. The authors use general data and provide results based on experiential simulations.

2 Professional Examination and Decision-Making in the Appraisal of Research Projects: Model Assumptions

The structure of the scientific community in Russia is heterogeneous. It is conditioned, on the one hand, by natural-geographical factors (particularly the spatial extent of the country), and on the other hand, by the intrinsic institutional features inherent in the scientific community itself. Depending on the interests and position of the observer, one can identify the following within the landscape of the scientific community: (a) institutional macroeconomic agents such as the Russian Academy of Sciences (RAS), Ministry of Science and Higher Education of the Russian Federation, scientific foundations (RFBR, RSF); (b) microeconomic level agents – universities, institutes of the Russian Academy of Sciences, private educational institutions, publishing houses of scientific literature; (c) agents of nanoeconomic level – individual scientists and their small groups (associations). At the same time, agents, regardless of what level of the economy they belong to, are endowed with a wide range of characteristics that influence their decision-making processes.

In this paper, which is devoted to the analysis of competitive financing mechanisms and professional examination of research projects, the authors focus on modeling the behavior of agents at the nanoeconomic level. Herewith we do not consider the relationship between the activities of agents of various levels in real life, (see for details on this aspect: [23]). Thus, in the proffered research model, there are two main types of objects: researchers (scientists) and research projects (works). Below is a description of the characteristics of these objects.

The first type of object are the researchers who make up the scientific community. Each researcher can either play the role of the producer of research projects (that are subject to decision-making by the scientific foundation on the question of financing), or the role of a reviewer – an expert who evaluates research projects submitted to the competition. The scientific community is heterogeneous: there are scientific schools in it, uniting both some performers and some reviewers. The results of project reviews may be influenced by the affiliation of the reviewer and the producer with one particular scientific school.

The basic economic and psychological characteristic of this type of object, whose influence on the examination processes of research projects we are interested in, is the oppositional binary "individualism – collectivism". Accounting for this characteristic in the model is carried out by assigning researchers to one of two disjointed sets: the class of dependent (collectivism) or the class of independent (individualism) researchers.

It is assumed that researchers in the first class (*dependent*) are influenced by the scientific school. Reviewers, in examining the research projects of producers related to the same scientific school, provide these producers with additional support, and overestimate their merits. Researchers belonging to the second class (*independent*), on the contrary, carry out a fair examination of the research projects of other researchers, regardless of the class in which the latter are included. In other words, if the reviewer is not a member of the scientific school, his rating does not depend on the affiliation of the project's producer to the scientific school.

Each researcher also possesses certain specific qualifications, has their own reputation, and feels a certain satisfaction or dissatisfaction from their activities. Qualification (*qualification*) affects the ability of the researcher to produce and examine research projects; reputation (*reputation*) reflects the degree of respect for this expert and the credibility of his opinion from the scientific community; and, satisfaction (*satisfaction*) shows the perception by the researcher of his position within the scientific community and his attitude to his reputation. These characteristics are randomly distributed among experts in the range from 0 to 1.

The second type of objects – research projects – are tied to the first type of objects – researchers. Each research project is characterized by two features: the value of the idea behind the project (*idea*) and the quality of its execution (*quality*). The value of the idea is set randomly in the range from 0 to 1. The quality of the execution of a research project is determined by the underlying idea and qualification of the researcher representing the project for the competition. Qualification determines his ability vis-a-vis the implementation of this idea: *quality* = *idea* · *qualification*. The quantity of research projects, both submitted for the competition and already carried out by researchers, is limited and does not exceed 50% of the total number of researchers. This provision reflects the necessity of taking into account the order of receipt of projects in the scientific foundations. Each researcher can submit only one project to the competition.

In the model proposed below, the process of research projects rating by dependent and independent experts is simulated. The duration of the simulation is limited to 100-time cycles, each of which is identified with a year. The population of researchers is not updated; the life expectancy of each researcher is assumed to be 100-time cycles. Choice of researchers submitting research projects for the competition, out of the total number of researchers, each tact takes place randomly, taking into account the restriction on the number of projects examined. Research projects that won the competition are executed during 3-time cycles.

3   Mechanisms for the Rating of Scientific Projects by Researchers, Realization of Feedback, and Conceptual Model Scheme

As mentioned above, the entire category of researchers in any individual time slot is divided into two equal parts – the producers of research (performers) and the review researchers. A researcher becomes a performer if his research project succeeds in the competitive process. In other words, some researchers are engaged in the preparation and implementation of research projects, while the other part rates the projects partic-ipating in the competition. The rating procedure is carried out in the following way: each project applying for funding is assigned a team of three randomly selected reviewers. As the researchers are divided into two classes – dependent and independent – we get four possible combinations of pairs within the category "reviewers of scientific project", each of which has its own assessment rules (see Table 1).

Table 1. Rules for examining research projects depending on the "class affiliation" of reviewers and producers of research projects.

Reviewer	Producer of research project	
	Dependent	Independent
Dependent	quality • qualification•(1 + 0.5 • opinion)	quality • qualification
Independent	quality • qualification	quality • qualification

The assessment of the first pair is implemented in the following way. The dependent reviewers seek to support the research projects of other researchers who are fellow members of their scientific school. Each dependent reviewer forms his opinion (opinion) on the project of another dependent researcher, with a value which is randomly set from 0 to 1. At the same time, the dependent reviewer cannot increase the final assessment of the research project by more than 50%, therefore, taking into account the opinion of the dependent reviewer, the assessment of the dependent researcher is formed in accordance with the formula *rate = quality • qualification • (1 + 0.5 • opinion)*. Thus, the compo-nent representing his personal attitude (subjectivity) is added to the reviewer's basic assessment (objectivity). A unified assessment system operates for the three remaining pairs: a research reviewer assesses the quality of a scientific project, based on his qualification *rate = quality · qualification*. If the final score of a scientific project *rate* by the reviewer is ≥ 0.6, then the variable result (which represents the decision to support the research project) is given 1 additional point. A scientific project is deemed to be supported in a case where the variable *result* has a value of ≥ 2, i.e. two reviewers out of three consider the project to be reasonably supported.

The mechanisms for changing the status of participants in the assessment after each slot are implemented through changes in the reputation and satisfaction of the researchers (see Table 2).

Table 2. Changing the satisfaction and reputation of researchers depending on winning or losing the competition.

Parameter	Reviewer	Producer of research projects			
		Dependent		Independent	
		(+)	(−)	(+)	(−)
Reputation	*Dependent*	0.3	X	0.5	X
	Independent	0.5	X	0.5	X
Satisfaction	*Any class*	0.3	−0.1	0.5	−0.1

In cases where a dependent producer wins the competition by means of the support provided by a dependent reviewer, the reputation of the scientific project producer increases by 0.3 points. If a scientific project wins the competition without additional support from dependent reviewers, then the reputation of the project producer increases by 0.5 points. For all researchers whose projects win the competition, satisfaction increases by 0.3 points, and for those whose projects were not supported, the reverse process takes place and the satisfaction value decreases by 0.1 points. At the same time, the reputation of the dependent reviewer is subject to change. If the scientific project of the dependent producer wins in the competition, then the reputation of the reviewer is reduced by 0.1 points, which represents the loss of confidence in him on behalf of the scientific community.

We also note that the reputation and satisfaction of researchers cannot fall below zero. In this case, the researcher is considered satisfied if the parameter for *satisfaction* is >0.

Accounting for the psychological characteristics of agents not only allows for the modeling of the project rating results in a more accurate manner, but also the discovery of new psychological structures in the scientific community. These structures arise in connection with a change in the estimated indicators of the researchers' activity, and adds to the characterization of their reputation (and the satisfaction of the current situation in the scientific community) after each slot. Based on these indicators, the researchers are arranged in small groups that can provide the most pleasant psychological atmosphere and comfort for the researcher. This matter is concerned with the formation of peculiar groups of "friends" ("neighbors") surrounding each researcher in the "satisfaction – reputation" space. Initially, such groups (numbering between four to nine researchers) are formed randomly. Depending on the situation, the researcher may try to choose another environment for himself and leave his group.

If a researcher is satisfied with his current position in the scientific community, his *satisfaction* value is >0, and he maintains his membership in this group. If a researcher is not satisfied with his current position in the scientific community, then his *satisfaction* value = 0, and he conducts an analysis of the participants reputation in his surrounding group. In cases when the total reputation of group members belonging to the same dependency class (independence) as the researcher is more than the total reputation value of the participants from another group, the researcher compares his reputation with the average reputation of all members of his environment. If the average reputation of the environment is lower than that of the unsatisfied researcher, his satisfaction increases by 0.1 points. Otherwise the researcher leaves his group and is seen to exist at large in the scientific space (whereby he finds other neighbors), and his satisfaction also increases by 0.1 points. In a situation where the total reputation of the neighbors belonging to the same class is less than the total reputation of the neighbors from another class, the researcher carries out a class change, i.e. the transfer from a set of dependent to a set of independent neighbors or vice versa, after which the satisfaction of the researcher also increases by 0.1 points. The scheme of the described examination model and the decision-making on the support of scientific projects is presented in Fig. 1.

4 Software Implementation of the Model and Analysis of the Results of Experimental Simulations

The tool for implementing the agent-based model is the Net Logo software package (environment), which is freely distributed and developed by Northwestern University (Northwestern University). More details about the advantages of this environment and its potential application in building models of natural, social and technical multi-agent systems can be found in the academic literature [24–26].

The interface of the model is presented in Fig. 2. In the left part of the interface, the control elements of the model are presented, the visualization of the virtual world is presented in the center, and the graphical information for analysis is on the right hand side.

The user has two available control levers, which are used to set the total number of researchers in the scientific community (*number*) and the proportion of researchers in the entire group belonging to the category of independents (*percent_independent*).

The virtual world is limited; agents cannot penetrate beyond its borders. The researchers (*scientists*) are presented in the form of large circles. Each researcher takes a specific place (cell, spot) in the virtual world, and two researchers cannot be in one place at the same time. The dependent class has a blue color; the independent class has a brown color. Researchers create research projects that take the form of small circles. Scientific projects that submitted for the competitions are marked in yellow, scientific projects that won the competition are in red.

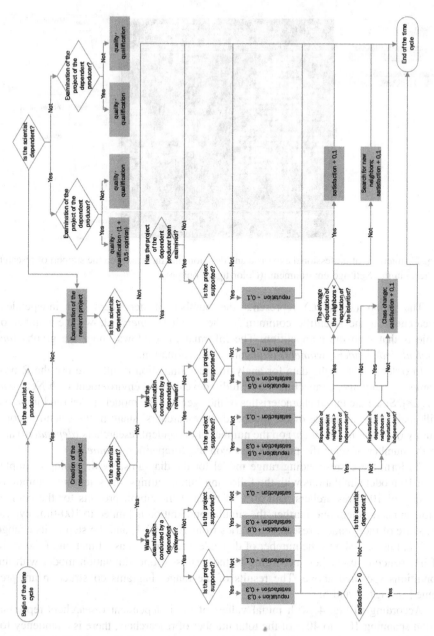

Fig. 1. Scheme of the model of examination and decision-making on the support of scientific projects.

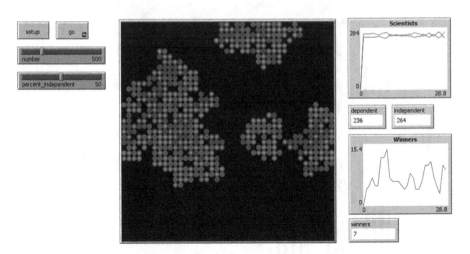

Fig. 2. Interface of professional expertise and decision-making model on the support of research projects in the NetLogo environment. (Color figure online)

The graph (*scientists*) represents the number of dependent and independent researchers in the scientific community; the graph (*winners*) shows the number of projects that won the competition. The information windows under the graphs (*dependent, independent, winners*) duplicate this information.

In order to obtain the data for analyzing the simulation results, we use the R programming language, connecting the RStudio development environment with Net Logo [27, 28]. Since the initial characteristics of the agents in the model are set randomly, we will analyze the influence of the independent researchers' share in the scientific community (*percent_independent*) on the number of dependent researchers (*dependent*) and on the number of scientific projects that won the competition (*winners*).

To form the corresponding range model for the diagrams, we are going to implement 10 model simulations with the following initial settings: the scientific community consists of 1000 researchers, and 50% of researchers submit projects for the competition and carry them out. Further, the simulation duration is limited to 100-time cycles, the share of independent researchers varies from 10 to 90%, and the step of its change is 10%. Figure 3 shows the number of dependent researchers as a function of the share of independent researchers according to the results of one simulation model with the conditions specified above. The results of the range diagrams construction are presented in Figs. 4 and 5.

According to Fig. 4, with initial values of the independent researchers representation spanning 10% to 40% of the total number of researchers, there is a tendency for independent researchers to become dependent. Upon completion of 100-time cycles, between 95% and 100% of researchers belong to the dependent class. A similar situation is observed with initial values of the independent researchers share of representation equal to from 60% to 90%. In this case, the reverse trend is visible - dependent researchers gravitate toward the independent category. By the completion of 100-time cycles, between 90% and 100% of researchers belong to the independent class.

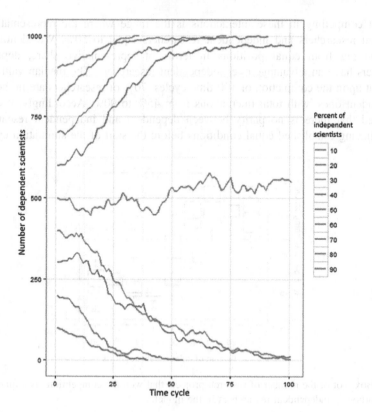

Fig. 3. Graph of the number of dependent scientists as a function of the proportion of independent researchers in the model.

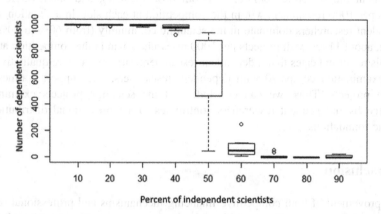

Fig. 4. Box plot of the number of dependent scientists as a function of the proportion of independent researchers in the model.

Most compelling in these interactions is the range where the representation of dependent researchers and independent researchers equal to 50%. We identify that when starting from equal positions in terms of representative share, dependent researchers have an advantage over independent researchers. The median value indicates that upon the completion of 100-time cycles, 70% of researchers are in the class of dependent ones, with total fluctuations from 45% to 90%. Accordingly, it can be concluded that there is no parity between dependent and independent researchers, despite having established equal conditions before the start of the simulation cycle.

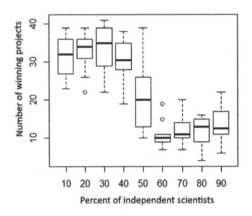

Fig. 5. Box plot of the number of research projects that won the competition, as a function of the proportion of independent researchers in the model.

We can draw the following conclusion based on Fig. 5. Dependent researchers dominate in the scientific community (from 60% to 90%), and about 33 research projects per 1000 researchers win in the competition at each slot. In a situation where independent researchers dominate in the scientific community (from 60% to 90%), on average, about 11 research projects per 1000 researchers win in the competition at each slot. This result indicates that independent researchers carry out a more qualitative and tough examination compared with dependent researchers, and support 3 times less research projects. Thus, we can conclude that the scientific projects examination conducted by independent researchers contributes to a more rational distribution of scientific foundations.

5   Conclusion

The improvement of both competitive financing mechanisms and professional review processes is a key task for the scientific and expert community. The agent-based model of professional expertise and decision-making on the support of scientific projects described in this paper, allows for the identification of the influence of certain economic and psychological characteristics of the researchers based on the results of competitive financing from the research funds. It is shown that such economic and psychological opposition, such as "individualism – collectivism", significantly affects the results of competitions. If the number of dependent researchers (who follow the interests of a certain group – 'collectivism'), dominates in the scientific community, so will a greater number of research projects receive financial support. In the reverse situation, where independent researchers dominate in the scientific community, the examination processes of scientific projects become more rigid and, accordingly, scientific foundations support fewer scientific projects. These circumstances allow us to match up researchers who criticize the anonymous public review method (*peer review*). The lack of accounting for the economic and psychological characteristics of reviewers who assess scientific projects significantly reduces the quality of this method. As a possible solution to this problem, along with the multistage methods that are currently used to conduct expert evaluations of scientific projects, we propose to take into account such characteristics by forming psychological profiles of reviewers. In other words, each expert, on the one hand, should have sufficient qualifications to conduct examinations of scientific projects, and on the other hand, should have a suitable psychological profile.

The results obtained in this research summarise the problems of organizing the examination of not only scientific, but also other socially significant initiatives in the situations where the majority forms public opinion about one or another initiative. These include, for example, the organization of public hearings, various kinds of contests, elections, public positions, etc. At the same time, the influence of the economic and psychological characteristics of agents will probably be significant too. By slightly changing the conditions of the constructed agent-based model, it can be applied to the study of a variety of such situations.

Currently, the agent-based model of professional expertise and decision-making on the support of scientific projects has a number of limitations, which we hope will be overcome in the future. In particular, the following areas can be highlighted to improve the model:

(a) considering the rationality (bounded rationality, up to irrationality) of the behavior of agents. Here, the mechanism of optimal decisions making by an agent in accordance with its rationality (bounded rationality, irrationality), taking into account the relation of this agent to restrictions in the area of making possible decisions may be realized;

(b) changing the agents' qualifications depending on the examinations to be carried out and the research projects submitted for the competition (economic and psychological opposition "reflection – antireflexia");

(c) taking into account the attitude of the researcher to his surroundings (economic and psychological opposition "introversion – extraversion");

(d) considering the possibility of examining scientific projects to the researchers who carry out and submit projects for the competition, without a formal division into the roles of producers and reviewers;

(e) providing an opportunity to simultaneously submit projects to the competition and engage in several research projects for the researchers;

(f) increasing the maximum number of agents in the simulation, which requires large computational power;

(g) updating the population of agents according to their age.

Solving these problems will help to improve the predictive abilities of the model and assist it in future predictions of operating results of multi-agent autonomous socio-economic systems.

References

1. Science Indicators: 2018: statistical compilation. National Research University "Higher School of Economics", p. 320. HSE, Moscow (2018) (in Russian)
2. Mindeli, L.E., Chernykh, S.I.: Funding of basic research in Russia: modern realities and forecasts. Stud. Russ. Econ. Dev. **27**(3), 318–325 (2016)
3. Ganguli, I.: Saving soviet science: the impact of grants when government R&D funding disappears. Am. Econ. J.: Appl. Econ. **9**(2), 165–201 (2017). https://doi.org/10.1257/app. 20160180
4. Federal Research and Development Funding: FY2018 Congressional Research Service, 25 January. https://fas.org/sgp/crs/misc/R44888.pdf. Accessed 30 Apr 2019 (2018)
5. Ilina, I.E., Zharova, E.N., Burlankov, S.P.: Analysis of the efficacy of public spending on research and development in state programs. Stud. Russ. Econ. Dev. **29**(2), 207–213 (2018)
6. Lee, C.J., Sugimoto, C.R., Zhang, G., Cronin, B.: Bias in peer review. J. Am. Soc. Inform. Sci. Technol. **64**(1), 2–17 (2013). https://doi.org/10.1002/asi.22784
7. Walker, R., da Silva, P.R.: Emerging trends in peer review—a survey. Front. Neurosci. **9**, 169 (2015). https://doi.org/10.3389/fnins.2015.00169
8. García, J.A., Rodriguez-Sánchez, R., Fdez-Valdivia, J.: Bias and effort in peer review. J. Assoc. Inform. Sci. Technol. **66**(10), 2020–2030 (2015). https://doi.org/10.1002/asi.23307
9. Morey, R.D., et al.: The peer reviewers' openness initiative: incentivizing open research practices through peer review. Roy. Soc. Open Sci. **3**(1), 150547 (2016). https://doi.org/10. 1098/rsos.150547
10. Mutz, R., Bornmann, L., Daniel, H.D.: Does gender matter in grant peer review? Zeitschrift für Psychol. **220**(2), 121–129 (2012). https://doi.org/10.1027/2151-2604/a000103
11. Fortin, J.M., Currie, D.J.: Big science vs. little science: how scientific impact scales with funding. PloS One **8**(6), e65263 (2013). https://doi.org/10.1371/journal.pone.0065263
12. Rijcke, S.D., Wouters, P.F., Rushforth, A.D., Franssen, T.P., Hammarfelt, B.: Evaluation practices and effects of indicator use—a literature review. Res. Eval. **25**(2), 161–169 (2016). https://doi.org/10.1093/reseval/rvv038
13. Bollen, J., Crandall, D., Junk, D., Ding, Y., Börner, K.: An efficient system to fund science: from proposal review to peer-to-peer distributions. Scientometrics **110**(1), 521–528 (2017). https://doi.org/10.1007/s11192-016-2110-3
14. Li, D., Agha, L.: Big names or big ideas: do peer-review panels select the best science proposals? Science **348**(6233), 434–438 (2015). https://doi.org/10.1126/science.aaa0185
15. Rennie, D.: Let's make peer review scientific. Nat. News **535**(7610), 31 (2016). https://doi. org/10.1038/535031a
16. Wicherts, J.M.: Peer review quality and transparency of the peer-review process in open access and subscription journals. PLoS One **11**(1), e0147913 (2016). https://doi.org/10. 1371/journal.pone.0147913
17. Squazzoni, F., Grimaldo, F., Marušić, A.: Publishing: journals could share peer-review data. Nature **546**(7658), 352 (2017)
18. Gropp, R.E., Glisson, S., Gallo, S., Thompson, L.: Peer review: a system under stress. Bioscience **67**(5), 407–410 (2017). https://doi.org/10.1093/biosci/bix034

19. Roumbanis, L. Peer review or lottery? A critical analysis of two different forms of decision-making mechanisms for allocation of research grants. Sci. Technol. Hum. Values. 0162243918822744 (2019). https://doi.org/10.1177/0162243918822744

20. Makarov, V.L., Bakhtizin, A.R., Sushko, E.D.: Simulation of population's reproductive behaviour patterns within an agent-oriented regional model. R-Economy **1**(3), 478–486 (2015)

21. Makarov, V.L., Bakhtizin, A.R., Sushko, E.D., Vasenin, V.A., Borisov, V.A., Roganov, V.A.: Supercomputer technologies in social sciences: agent-oriented demographic models. Herald Russ. Acad. Sci. **86**(3), 248–257 (2016)

22. Kulivets, S.G., Ushakov, D.V.: Modeling relationship between cognitive abilities and economic achievements. Psychol. J. High. School Econ. **13**(4), 636–648 (2016)

23. Oleinik, A.: Knowledge and Networking: On Communication in the Social Sciences, p. 238. Transaction Publishers, New Brunswick (2014). https://doi.org/10.4324/9780203787670

24. Wilensky, U., Rand, W.: An Introduction to Agent-Based Modeling: Modeling Natural, Social, and Engineered Complex Systems with NetLogo. The MIT Press, Cambridge (2015). 504 p

25. Banitz, T., Gras, A., Ginovart, M.: Individual-based modeling of soil organic matter in NetLogo: transparent, user-friendly, and open. Environ. Model Softw. **71**, 39–45 (2015)

26. Gaudou, B., Lang, C., Marilleau, N., Savin, G., Coyrehourcq, S.R., Nicod, J.M.: Netlogo, an open simulation environment. In: Agent-based Spatial Simulation with NetLogo, vol. 2, pp. 1–36. IS TE – Elsevier, London (2017)

27. Thiele, J.C.: R marries NetLogo: introduction to the RNetLogo package. J. Stat. Softw. **58**(2), 1–41 (2014)

28. Thiele, J.C., Grimm, V.: NetLogo meets R: linking agent-based models with a toolbox for their analysis. Environ. Model Softw. **25**(8), 972–974 (2010)

Agent-Based-Model of Students' Sociocognitive Learning Process in Acquiring Tiered Knowledge

Ismo T. Koponen$^{(\boxtimes)}$ (iD)

Department of Physics, University of Helsinki, Helsinki, Finland
ismo.koponen@helsinki.fi

Abstract. The cognitive and social aspects of students' learning process in acquiring scientific, tiered system of knowledge are explored by using an agent-based-model. Cognitive aspects of learning are described as foraging for the best explanations on epistemic landscapes, whose tiered structures are set by instructional design. The sociodynamic aspects of learning are described as an agent-based model, where agents compare and adjust their proficiency through peer-to-peer comparisons. The results show that even in cases where social learning is unbiased, social learning has a substantial effect on learning outcomes.

Keywords: Sociocognitive learning · Agent-based-model ·
Epistemic landscape

1 Introduction

Students' learning processes for acquiring advanced and abstract scientific knowledge are complicated ones, with cognitive and social learning playing crucial roles [1–3]. Such learning processes have been discussed from viewpoints based on complex dynamic systems [3–5], where the cognitive and social aspect of learning [1,6] are seen in equally important roles. In that learning process, two key issues are: First, learner's mental models and explanatory schemes are strongly context dependent [2,3], giving emergence to varied but robust outcomes within a given context [4,5], and second, social learning may significantly boost learning even in cases where only indirect effects operate through constant peer-to-peer comparisons which reinforce students' self-efficacy [6] or mutual appreciation [7].

Here, an agent-based-model is introduced for exploring the social and cognitive aspects of teaching-learning processes, referred briefly as the *sociocognitive* aspects of learning. The target system to be modelled here is a five-person group, with a learning task to learn a tiered system of explanatory schemes to explain a set of observed phenomena, for which only a few possible explanatory schemes of different levels of sophistication are available, corresponding to some well-known and extensively studied cases of learning scientific knowledge [4,5]. The basic assumptions in modelling such a teaching-learning process are that the process

© Springer Nature Switzerland AG 2019
N. Agarwal et al. (Eds.): MSBC 2019, CCIS 1079, pp. 82–95, 2019.
https://doi.org/10.1007/978-3-030-29862-3_7

is affected by: (1) the context of learning and its design, (2) students' cognitive abilities and proficiencies, and (3) social interactions. These three *sociocognitive* aspects and how they are idealised are discussed in more detail in what follows. The teaching-learning task and the corresponding explanatory schemes are modelled as an epistemic landscape [8,9] while the cognitive dynamics of learning is described as the agent's exploration of the epistemic landscape. Social interactions, on the other hand, are modelled by using an agent-based model of how agents' proficiencies develop solely through their mutual comparisons of their proficiencies [10].

2   Models of Knowledge and Learning

Knowledge systems which are the target of learning of interest here are systems of tiered knowledge schemes [4,5]. A concrete example of such system consist of explanatory schemes describing the behaviour of simple DC-circuits, where from five to seven explanatory schemes can be discerned [4,5]. Consequently, a three-tiered system consisting of five explanatory schemes $m_1 - m_5$ is assumed here. The details of the tiered systems and how they correspond to real learning tasks are explained elsewhere [5].

Each scheme $m_1 - m_5$ can be associated with a utility function u_k, with $k = 1, \ldots 5$, which provides an abstract representation of the likelihood that scheme m_k provides an explanation. The utility u_k depends on two external (exogenous) variables ϵ and κ. The first variable $\epsilon \in [0, 1]$ is the relative number of explained features (i.e. explanans) contained in tasks. The value $\epsilon = 1$ describes the explanandum, where all features are explained and the explanans becomes equal to the explanandum. The second variable is the proficiency $\kappa \in [0, 1]$, which describes the proficiency required from a learner to use a given scheme m_k in providing explanations. The value $\kappa = 1$ denotes full mastery in using the highest-level schemes [10].

Explanatory schemes have different utilities in different situations of explanation. Using or not using the given scheme is assumed to depend on its utility in a given context or situation and the proficiency of the user, higher level schemes requiring higher proficiency. The tiered system of explanatory schemes can be described by constructing a corresponding manifold of utility functions, called an epistemic landscape (see refs. [8,9] and the references therein). The system of utility functions is modelled here as a set of Gaussian functions in a two-dimensional space (ϵ, κ) spanned by the explanans $\epsilon \in [0, 1]$ and proficiency $\kappa \in [0, 1]$, in form

$$u_k(\epsilon, \kappa) = \exp[-(\frac{1}{2(1 - \rho^2)}(\frac{(\epsilon - \epsilon_k)^2}{2w_\epsilon^2} + \frac{(\kappa - \kappa_k)^2}{2w_\kappa^2}) + 2\rho\frac{(\epsilon - \epsilon_k)(\kappa - \kappa_k)}{w_\epsilon w_\kappa})] \quad (1)$$

where ϵ_k and κ_k define the maximum, with $\epsilon_{k+1} > \epsilon_k$ and $\kappa_{k+1} > \kappa_k$ corresponding to the tiering of schemes m_k. The allowed variation in utility is governed by w_ϵ and w_κ, respectively, while ρ controls the (positive) correlation between proficiency and explanans, taken here to be only moderate with $\rho = 0.20$.

The fact that explanatory schemes contain similar elements means that learning one scheme may help or hinder learning a closely related scheme. Such entanglement of the explanatory schemes $m_1 - m_5$ is here described at an idealised, generative level, by using an entanglement factor which modifies the schemes so that utility functions u'_k affected by entanglement are given by (compare with ref. [11])

$$\tilde{u}_k = u_k(1 + \Delta_k \Theta), \quad \text{where} \sum_k \Delta_k = 0 \tag{2}$$

where $\Theta = \sum_k u_k \cos\left[(\pi R_k)/(2\lambda)\right]$ with $R_k = [(\epsilon - \epsilon_k)^2 + (\kappa - \kappa_k)^2]^{1/2}$ models the effects of entanglement. The parameter λ is roughly related to the number of combinatorial factors responsible for the entanglement and thus affects the number of intermediate maxima in the entangled landscape between maxima in the non-entangled landscape. The entanglement factor Δ_k for the utility functions are defined as $D_1 = A_{1,2} + A_{1,3}$, $D_2 = -A_{1,2} + A_{2,3}$, $D_3 = -A_{1,3} - A_{2,3} + A_{3,4} + A_{3,5}$, $D_4 = -A_{3,4} - A_{3,5} + A_{4,5}$ and $D_5 = -A_{4,5}$, where $A_{k,k'} = A_0\sqrt{u_k u_{k'}}$. The entanglement factors sum up to zero so that they only redistributes the probability mass. Three different epistemic landscapes A-C studied here are shown in Fig. 1.

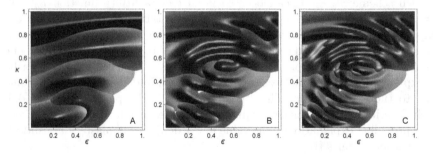

Fig. 1. The epistemic landscape in two dimensional space spanned by explanans ϵ and proficiency κ and consisting of utilities u_1 (orange), u_2 (blue), u_3 (green), u_4 (purple) and u_5 (red). The three different landscape models shown are: A (no entanglement), B ($\lambda = 3$) and C ($\lambda = 5$). (Color figure online)

Cognitive learning is described by a probabilistic learning model (PLM), where the most probable scheme is selected through comparison of utilities u_k so that the selection of a given explanatory scheme m_k follow a simple canonical probability distribution [10–12]

$$P(m_k) = \left[1 + \sum_{j \neq k} \exp\left[-\beta(\tilde{u}_k - \tilde{u}_j) \right] \right]^{-1} \tag{3}$$

with utilities $\tilde{u}_k$ given by Eq. (2). The parameter β determines the noise-level of selection and is termed in what follows the *confidence* of choice. In what follows, only high confidence choices with $\beta = 10$ are considered, corresponding in practice to all choices with $\beta \gg 1$.

The foraging on the epistemic landscape consists now of τ attempts to find the best explaining scheme. In practice, the number of attempts is chosen to be $\tau_{\mathrm{MAX}} = 15 \times 12$ corresponding to 15 attempts for each key feature. This is enough to reach stable final states and stable LOAs in the simulations. At each instant when the value of τ is increased by one event, it is decided:

1. which scheme m_k becomes selected
2. what is the explanans provided by m_k
3. how proficiency κ changes as guided by m_k

Each of these three steps is characterized by a set of probabilities and the selection of an outcome is carried out on the basis of the "roulette wheel" method [13]. In this method a discrete set of possible outcomes $k = 1, 2, \ldots, N$ with probabilities Π_k are arranged cumulatively with cumulative probability $\Phi_k = (\sum_{j' \leq k} \Pi_{j'}) / \sum_{j' \leq N} \Pi_{j'}$. The outcome k is selected if a random number $r* \in [0, 1]$ falls in the slot $\Phi_{k-1} < r* < \Phi_k$, where $\Phi_0 = 0$. In case (1) the probabilities Π_k are given by Eq. (5) with $k = 1, \ldots, 5$ for all five possible choices. In cases (2) and (3) Π_k is given by marginal probability distributions $U_\kappa(k = \kappa*) = \int u_k(\kappa*, \epsilon)d\epsilon$ and $U_\epsilon(k = \epsilon*) = \int u_k(\kappa, \epsilon*)d\kappa$, where $\epsilon*$ and $\kappa*$ are discretised to $k \in [1, 100]$ discrete bins. The values of $\epsilon*$ and $\kappa*$ sampled from the marginal distribution U_ϵ and U_κ represent the agent's new attempted explanans and proficiency, which may be larger or smaller than the initial ones. However, the agent is not assumed to change its state independent of its current state. Instead, the change of state depends on how agent's attempted new state at $\tau+1$ is related to its initial state at τ. The realised changes are calculated from a discretised evolution equation for explanans ϵ and proficiency κ as follows

$$\epsilon_{\tau+1} \leftarrow \epsilon_\tau + \delta\epsilon \tag{4}$$

$$\kappa_{\tau+1} \leftarrow \kappa_\tau + \mu\,\delta\kappa\,[4\kappa_\tau(1 - \kappa_\tau)] \tag{5}$$

The changes $\delta\epsilon$ and $\delta\kappa$ depend on the sign of change where $\delta\epsilon$ and $\delta\kappa$ depend on the state of the agent and on the attempted new state as shown in Table 1. The evolution Eq. (5), where in the equation for κ parameter μ is the memory

Table 1. Changes $\delta\epsilon$ and $\delta\kappa$ in explanans and proficiency, respectively, to be used in the evolution equations for agent's state changes in Eqs. (4)–(5). The initial values are ϵ and κ and the new attempted values sampled from marginal distributions U_ϵ and U_κ) are $\epsilon*$ and $\kappa*$.

δu_k	$\delta\epsilon$		$\delta\kappa$	
	$\epsilon* \geq \epsilon$	$\epsilon* < \epsilon$	$\kappa* \geq \kappa$	$\kappa* < \kappa$
$\delta u_k \geq 0$	$\epsilon* - \epsilon$	$\epsilon* - \epsilon$	$u_k(\tau+1)(\kappa* - \kappa)$	$u_k(\tau)(\kappa* - \kappa)$
$\delta u_k < 0$	$u_k(\tau+1)(\epsilon* - \epsilon)$	0	$u_k(\tau+1)(\kappa* - \kappa)$	$u_k(\tau)(\kappa* - \kappa)$

effect and the term $4\kappa(1-\kappa)$ takes into account the cognitive limits in changes of proficiency, leads to logistic evolution of the proficiency [10]. Regarding the explanans, the above rule means that the utility function decides how much in a given stage τ of the exploration (or foraging) agent manages to explain, given its current state i.e. proficiency κ and adopted explanatory scheme m_k. Regarding proficiency, the above rules implement the idea that if evolution is in the direction of stronger explanations, then the proficiency κ increases, but if the direction is on the weaker explanations, corresponding to failure, then proficiency κ decreases. Such cognitive dynamics can be also interpreted as a "hill climbing" –type of exploration of an epistemic landscape [8]. The parameter μ controls the strength of the memory of success or failure. In principle it can be different for success and failure, but in what follows, for want of better information, we discuss only the case of equal memory for success and failure.

Proficiency is here not considered as a fixed property, but depending on peer-to-peer comparison and appraisals between peers [10] (see also refs. [6,7]). The dynamic equations for the proficiency are thus assumed to follow a bounded confidence model [10,14,15]. In that model, the changes in proficiency due to interaction between agents q and q' with possession of explanatory schemes m_k and m'_k and proficiencies κ and κ', respectively, are given by

$$\kappa \leftarrow \kappa + \gamma\, J_{q,q'}(\kappa' - \kappa)[4\,\kappa(1-\kappa)] \tag{6}$$

$$\kappa' \leftarrow \kappa' + \gamma\, J_{q,q'}(\kappa - \kappa')[4\,\kappa'(1-\kappa')] \tag{7}$$

where $J_{q,q'} = \exp\left[-(\sqrt{(k'/5)}\,\kappa' - \sqrt{(k/5)}\,\kappa)^2/(2\sigma^2)\right]\exp\left[-(\epsilon' - \epsilon)^2/(2\sigma^2)\right]$ is the propagator for the change (compare with ref. [14,15]). The width σ of the Gaussian function is related to the agents' tolerance to diversity (the *diversity* in what follows) in proficiency. In the simulations $\gamma = 0.15$, chosen to represent moderate sensitivity, is kept fixed, and only the parameter σ is changed. The output variables of the simulations are the agents' proficiencies and the relative number density $n_k(\epsilon, \kappa)$ of adopted explanatory scheme m_k in the space spanned by proficiency κ and explanans ϵ. Because κ evolves during the simulations, this leads eventually to accumulation of scheme choices, seen as peaked values of $n_k(\epsilon, \kappa)$ at certain regions in the (ϵ, κ)-space. These regions, in what follows, are called Learning Outcome Attractors or LOAs.

The LOAs and their evolution during the simulations when explorations on the epistemic landscape increases with increasing value of τ provides, however, very detailed information of the evolution of the agents' states. A more compact measure is provided simply as an integral measure of the total (relative) number density N_k of a given explanatory scheme m_k, in the form

$$N_k = N_0^{-1}\int n_k(\epsilon, \kappa)d\epsilon d\kappa, \tag{8}$$

with the normalisation N_0 chosen so that $\sum_k N_k = 1$. The total number density N_k is then used to track the learning process.

3   Results

The dynamic systems model, which describes learning as foraging for knowledge on an epistemic landscape, leads to the formation of robust learning outcomes attractors (LOAs), where learning paths accumulate. The formation of the LOAs is determined by the interplay of learning by foraging for knowledge on the epistemic landscape and by social learning. Here, the focus is on social learning and on the effects the entangled and overlapping components of explanatory schemes have on learning. In order to keep the social learning effects and entanglement effects in control, we have chosen here to keep the parameters β, μ and γ fixed, a corresponding high confidence ($\beta = 10$) in selection of explanatory schemes, low cognitive learning ($\mu = 0.05$) and moderate sensitivity to social learning ($\gamma = 0.15$). In addition, we study only one type of cohort of learners, where all the learners have low initial proficiency $0.05 < \kappa < 0.25$. This cohort is the most interesting one and shows the most nontrivial behaviour in regard to learning, thus best revealing the effects of social learning.

The learning outcome attractors (LOAs) resulting from cognitive learning and social learning are shown in Fig. 2 for epistemic landscape C for three diversities $\sigma = 0.08, 0.10$ and 0.14 and for an increased number of exploration attempts $\tau = 0.05, 0.15, 0.40$ and 1.00. The results are shown as density distributions $n_k(\epsilon, \kappa)$ of preferred explanatory schemes in the end of the learning sequence corresponding to $\tau = 1$ The shift to select more advanced schemes during the learning when τ increases from $\tau = 0.15$ (little exploration) to $\tau = 1$ (exploration to nearly saturation) is particularly clear when a density from $n_k(\epsilon, \kappa)$- of selected explanatory scheme in the (κ, ϵ)-space is examined.

The results in Fig. 2 show that by increasing the tolerance to diversity σ in social learning, the outcomes of learning are significantly improved. Interactions with more competent peers, although they do not directly nor proportionally increase the agent's proficiency, increases the rate of growth of proficiency. In all these cases, however, the LOAs are located roughly in areas of (ϵ, κ) -space, where the epistemic landscape has peak values, but the details of formation of LOAs depend on diversity and entanglement. In practice this would mean that very different learning outcomes are observed depending on how extensively learner's explore the tasks (described by τ) and how tolerant they are to their peers' diversities in proficiency (described by σ). For shallow exploration (low values of τ) and low tolerance to diversity, i.e. high homophily (low values of σ), learning outcomes may appear better in comparison to cases when diversity is high. However, when chances for exploration and thus for interaction are increased (increasing value of τ), learning outcomes become better for cases where tolerance to diversity is high; given enough time for explorations and interactions, interactions with peers is always beneficial even in the absence of bias to learn from more competent peers. This is an outcome of how exploration of the epistemic landscape, its structure, and social learning are interconnected. In practice, it means interconnections between task structure (designed to advance learning) and collaborative learning where learners communicate with their peers. It is

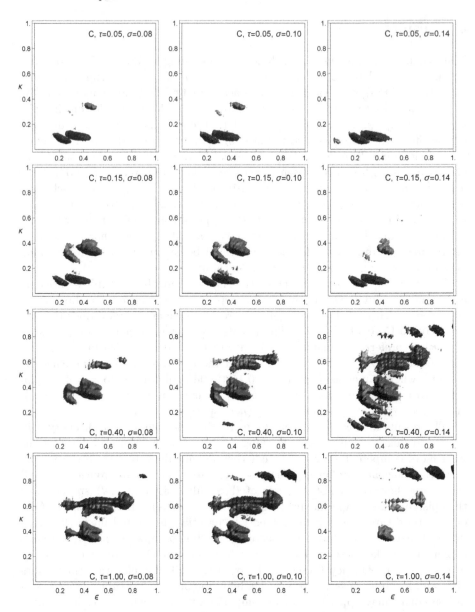

Fig. 2. The Learning Outcome Attractors (LOAs) for epistemic landscape C. The LOAs are recognised as peaked regions in number density distribution $n_k(\epsilon, \kappa)$ for schemes m_k, shown as: n_1 (orange), n_2 (blue), n_3 (green), n_4 (purple) and n_5 (red). The results are shown at different stages of evolution and for different values of diversity σ, as indicated in panels. Only densities $n_k > 0.1$ are shown. The darker/lighter shade indicates positive/negative gradients of n_k. (Color figure online)

noteworthy that the advantageous effect of competent peers persists even if the strength γ of social learning is fixed and only the diversity σ changes.

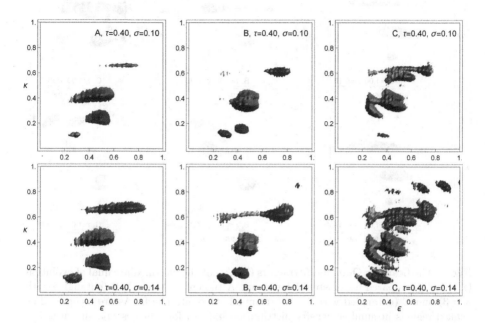

Fig. 3. The Learning Outcome Attractors (LOAs) at the intermediate stage of evolution ($\tau = 0.40$) compared for epistemic landscape A (no entanglement), B (entangled with $\lambda = 3$) and C (entangled with $\lambda = 5$), from left to right. The LOAs are recognised as peaked regions in number density distribution $n_k(\epsilon, \kappa)$ for schemes m_k, shown as: n_1 (orange), n_2 (blue), n_3 (green), n_4 (purple) and n_5 (red). The results are shown for an intermediate stage of evolution $\tau = 0.40$ and for diversity $\sigma = 0.10$ (upper panels) and $\sigma = 0.14$ (lower panels), as indicated in panels. Only densities $n_k > 0.1$ are shown. The darker/lighter shade indicates positive/negative gradients of n_k. (Color figure online)

The effect of entanglement in LOAs is shown in Fig. 3 for models A (no entanglement), B (entangled with $\lambda = 3$) and C (entangled with $\lambda = 5$) an intermediate stage of evolution, and for final states in Fig. 4. The effect of entanglement is also detectable, although it is clearly weaker than the effect of diversity. In Fig. 3 we see that for intermediate diversity the non-entangled landscape A leads to the formation of very sharply defined LOAs, and even the LOA corresponding scheme m_4 and high proficiency is formed. In the entangled landscapes B and C equally, strong LOAs corresponding m_4 and m_5 of high proficiency emerge only when high explanans values ϵ are reached. In practice, this means that if only low values of ϵ (corresponding to relatively simple situations and only a moderate number of observations to be explained), non-entangled model A provides better learning outcomes in comparison to entangled cases B and C. In all cases, however, the diversity increases learning. Interestingly, the highly entangled model

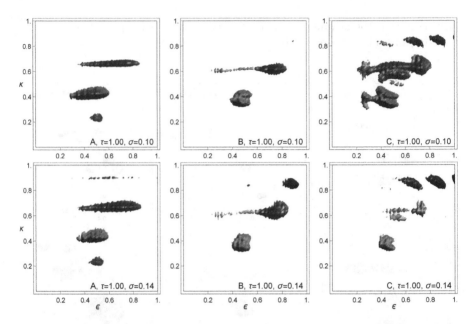

Fig. 4. The Learning Outcome Attractors (LOAs) at the intermediate final of evolution ($\tau = 1.00$) compared for epistemic landscape A (no entanglement), B (entangled with $\lambda = 3$) and C (entangled with $\lambda = 5$), from left to right. The LOAs are recognised as peaked regions in number density distribution $n_k(\epsilon, \kappa)$ for schemes m_k, shown as: n_1 (orange), n_2 (blue), n_3 (green), n_4 (purple) and n_5 (red). The results are shown for an intermediate stage of evolution $\tau = 0.40$ and for diversity $\sigma = 0.10$ (upper panels) and $\sigma = 0.14$ (lower panels), as indicated in panels. Only densities $n_k > 0.1$ are shown. The darker/lighter shade indicates positive/negative gradients of n_k. (Color figure online)

C with high diversity $\sigma = 0.14$ (Fig. 3 lower right) leads to the emergence of high proficiency LOAs already corresponding to scheme m_5 at intermediate stages of evolution and already for intermediate explanans with $\epsilon > 0.3$. This shows that appearance of states due to entanglement may help the very effective shift from lower level explanatory schmes to higher level ones if social learning facilitates this shift.

The interplay of entanglement and diversity in social learning is, however, rather complicated. When final, nearly stabilised LOAS corresponding $\tau = 1$ are examined, shown in Fig. 4, we observe that while diversity $\sigma = 0.10$ again leads clearly to better learning outcomes for entangled (B and C) than for non-entangled landscapes (A), this is no longer the case when diversity is high, having a value of $\sigma = 0.14$. Now, again, we see that the non-entangled model A gives emergence to sharply defined high proficiency LOAs for m_5 and for m_4. In fact, if learning outcomes only for $\epsilon < 0.7$ are examined (corresponding roughly to tasks I-III and omitting task IV) it appears that A outperforms B and C. The advantages of the entangled condition contained in B and C become evident only for $\epsilon > 0.7$, i.e. only when a complex enough task are involved.

In all cases we observe the strong presence of an LOA corresponding to m_3. This LOA is present and clearly visible also at the final stages for high diversity cases. Interestingly, the LOA corresponding to m_3 persists even when the LOA corresponding to m_4 begins to diminish, apparently feeding the LOA corresponding to m_5. This phenomenon, where at final stages and especially for high diversity, LOAs of m_3 and m_5 are the most persistent ones, shows that symmetric, non-biased and zero-average interaction of social learning and non-biased, zero average cognitive learning leads to the polarisation of learning outcomes. Many agents successfully reach the highest, high proficiency LOAs, but some agents are stuck forever at the final low LOAs with low proficiencies. This is, of course, an outcome of the bounded confidence type model adopting certain proficiency states, which, when formed, remain stable. This phenomenon corresponds to the resistance of learners to change their strong adherence in certain low level explanatory schemes irrespective of the fact that they do not explain but only a part of the observations they encounter in the given task (see e.g. [4,5]).

To get a more comprehensive picture of how social learning and differently entangled epistemic landscapes affect the agents' learning we need to condense the information contained in Figs. 2, 3 and 4. For this purpose, we use the total number density N_k of adoption of scheme m_k. The total number density N_k compresses the information of how a given explanatory scheme is learned into a single number, but no longer provide the information of explanans and proficiency contained in the LOAs. The results for different diversities from $\sigma=0.08$ to 0.18, for landscapes A, B and C and for $\tau \in [0,1]$ are shown in Fig. 5.

The results in Fig. 5 show that if one focuses only on simple tasks (tasks I-III, corresponding roughly $\epsilon < 0.7$) with low and moderate diversity ($\sigma = 0.08$ and 0.10), the non-entangled landscape A produces the best learning outcomes and scheme m_3 is rapidly learned. Only when the task becomes more demanding ($\epsilon > 0.7$), or when diversity increases ($\sigma > 0.10$), the entangled landscapes B and C become more advantageous for learning. On the other hand, the best learning outcomes are reached for entangled landscapes and high diversity $\sigma > 0.14$. In examining the results, it should be borne in mind that in all the cases the same value of memory μ of cognitive learning and strength γ of social learning has been kept constant. Also, the variations in probability mass contained is kept unbiased, with zero-averaged variation, in the same way as the tolerance to diversity in social learning which is also unbiased with zero-average variation.

The learning models of cognitive and social learning which produce these results are highly idealised, but, nevertheless, they show how delicately the learning outcomes depend on the interplay between task (as describe by epistemic landscapes) and the peer-to-peer interactions contained in social learning, and on the extension and duration (parameter τ) of exploration of the possible explanations (parameter ϵ). It is evident, that all the factors discussed here - cognitive learning, entanglement of different explanatory schemes, social learning, and tolerance to diversity - affect the learning outcomes, not only separately and independently but together as a whole system.

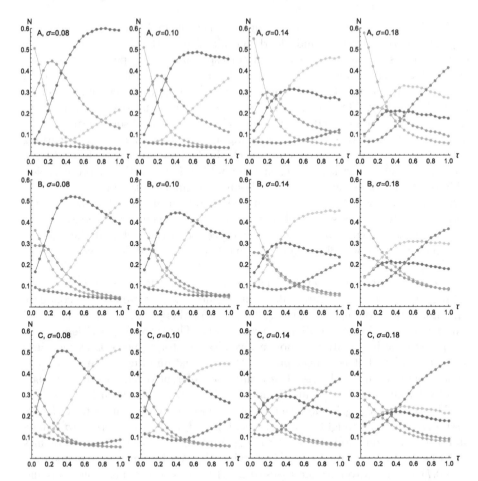

Fig. 5. The total number density of N_k for adoption of schemes m_k for epistemic landscape A (no entanglement), B (entangled with $\lambda = 3$) and C (entangled with $\lambda = 5$), from left to right. Total number densities $N_k(\epsilon, \kappa)$ for schemes m_k, shown as: N_1 (orange), N_2 (blue), N_3 (green), N_4 (purple) and N_5 (red). Results are shown for the complete stage of evolution from $\tau \in [0, 1]$ to and for diversity $\sigma = 0.08, 0.10, 0.14$ and 0.18. (Color figure online)

4   Discussion and Conclusions

The process of learning scientific knowledge from the dynamic systems viewpoint [4] is here discussed in terms of the Probabilistic Learning Model (PLM) for the cognitive effects of learning and in terms of a social learning model (SLM) for the effects of social interactions in learning [10]. The model of learning based on PLM and SLM is a sociocognitive model of learning, which considers some very primary features of a student's learning process on the levels of individual cognition and the sociodynamics of learning. The model is an idealised description of the learning process, based on the assumptions that: (1) the teaching-learning sequence can be described as an epistemic landscape; (2) the only relevant cognitive property that characterises the learner and changes during the teaching-learning sequence is the learners' proficiency in using the given scheme, enhanced/weakened by success/failure; and (3) social interaction either increases or decreases proficiency independently of cognitive abilities. In the present model, social learning is thus indirect instead of being a direct transfer of knowledge. This agrees with the views that social learning very often seems to operate through the indirect effect increasing the learners' self-efficacy and their feelings of competence [6,7].

The model of knowledge system studied here is a tiered system of explanatory schemes which is a generic description of certain well-known empirically studied learning situations (see e.g. [4,5]) and references therein). Sociocognitive dynamics, as it is implemented in the model, leads to the formation of dynamically robust preferences for certain explanatory schemes, which explains a set of evidence contained in the learning task designed to facilitate targeted learning. Adopting and using such explanatory schemes require appropriate proficiency from a learner. Thus, each explanatory scheme is characterised by what it explains (explanans) and what is the proficiency it requires from a learner. Robust learning outcomes can be then conceptualised as Learning Outcome Attractors (LOAs) corresponding to these schemes, located in space spanned by explanans and proficiency. These learning outcome attractors (LOAs) are essentially outcomes of the interplay between the design of the learning task, learners' cognitive dynamics and social dynamics.

The development and implementation the model shares many similarities with decision models and opinion dynamics models. The model is basically an agent-based model (ABM), where agents have an internal state characterised by the adopted explanatory scheme and proficiency. Both these features evolve during the simulations. The selection of interaction between agents is based on the bounded confidence type model. A similar type of social interaction has been recently proposed for modelling social interaction in the task centered collaboration [14]. The current model, in its use of epistemic landscapes, has also many similarities with simulation models designed for discovery of knowledge [8,9].

In the present model, the effects of social learning can account for a considerable part of successful learning and be comparable to cases where the memory effects (i.e. cognitive effect) in learning are high (see refs. [10]). Interestingly, although even in cases where the effect social learning depends on the difference between proficiencies and the positive and negative changes have similar effects, and even in case the probability for such events is without bias to positive effects, the effective outcome favours advancement in learning. This is due to the fact that the epistemic landscape itself, due to its design, is biased to advancement; positive change in proficiency matters more than equally strong negative change and learning bias emerges. This, of course, is due to fact that learning tasks, which the epistemic landscape is intended to model, is deliberately designed to support learning. The tolerance of diversity of peers' proficiencies thus allows learners to benefit occasionally with interaction with more competent peers and such cases are magnified by the effect it produces as an improved foraging capacity; the occasional encounter with more competent peers open new vistas for cognitive development. The social effect is thus not only restricted to adoption of peer's best choices but more importantly, it drives the agent's own cognitive proficiency. This result, although based on idealised model, suggest that tolerance to diversity of peers in social learning, when learning tasks are appropriately designed, is always beneficial for growth of proficiency, because it opens learning possibilities which may significantly enhance learning.

The results presented here have also implications for research into learning. In the picture presented here learning appears as a dynamic, continuous change from one dynamically and contextually determined learning outcome to another rather than a switch from one static, cognitively determined and context independent state to another. Research settings that can detect such a continuous change evolution and its context dependence of learning outcomes should pay attention to the effects of alternation between contexts and how interleaving of different contexts affect the learning outcomes. However, the complexity of the situation makes the mapping of the model parameters onto empirically testable research settings challenging. While proficiency can be mapped to success in providing correct answers in the given task (see e.g [4,5]), the tolerance to diversity, although in principle possible to operationalise in empirically accessible form, would require a novel types of reliable self-evaluation reports. Therefore, developing research settings which are appropriate for exploring rich variations of learning outcomes related to context dependence and how it interacts with learning dynamics remains thus as a challenge. In meeting such challenges and in advancing the research in sociocognitive learning the agent-based simulations may prove to be an invaluable tool. One advantage of the agent-based modelling as it is presented here is that the conceptualisation of learning within it is designed to be close to conceptualisations of social and collaborative learning phenomena now emerging in educational research of learning and instruction (see e.g. [16] and references therein). Complementing such research with agent-based modelling may eventually open new fruitful ways to model learning phenomena and to find new empirical approaches to study complex sociocognitive learning phenomena.

References

1. Amin, T.G., Smith, C.L., Wiser, M.: Student conceptions and conceptual change. In: Lederman, N.G., Abell, S.K. (eds.) Handbook of Reseach on Science Education, pp. 57–81. Routledge, New York (2014)
2. Gupta, A., Hammer, D., Redish, E.F.: The case for dynamic models of learners' ontologies in physics. J. Learn. Sci. **19**, 285–321 (2010)
3. Brown, D.E.: Students' conceptions as dynamically emergent structures. Sci. Educ. **23**, 1463–1483 (2014)
4. Koponen, I.T., Kokkonen, T.: A Systemic view of the learning and differentiation of scientific concepts: the case of electric current and voltage revisited. Frontline Learn. Res. **4**, 140–166 (2014)

5. Kokkonen, T., Mäntylä, T.: Changes in university students' explanation models of DC circuits. Res. Sci. Educ. **48**, 753–775 (2018)
6. Bandura, A.: Toward a psychology of human agency. Perspect. Psychol. Sci. **1**, 164–180 (2006)
7. Lawler, E.J.: An affect theory of social exchange. Am. J. Soc. **107**, 321–352 (2001)
8. McKenzie, A., Himmelreich, J., Thompson, C.: Epistemic landscapes, optimal search and the division of cognitive labor. Philos. Sci. **82**, 424–453 (2015)
9. Fernández Pinto, M., Fernández Pinto, D.: Epistemic landscapes reloaded: an examination of agent-based models in social epistemology. Hist. Soc. Res. **43**, 48–71 (2018)
10. Koponen, I.T., Kokkonen, T., Nousiainen, M.: Modelling sociocognitive aspects of students' learning. Phys. A **470**, 68–81 (2017)
11. Yukalov, V.I., Sornette, D.: Quantum probabilities as behavioral probabilities. Entropy **19**, 112 (2017)
12. Laciana, A.C., Oteiza-Aguirre, N.: An agent based multi-optional model for the diffusion of innovations. Phys. A **394**, 254–265 (2014)
13. Lipowski, A., Lipowska, D.: Roulette-wheel selection via stochastic acceptance. Phys. A **391**, 2193–2196 (2012)
14. Grow, A., Flache, A., Wittek, R.: An Agent-based model of status construction in task focused groups. J. Artif. Soc. Soc. Simul. **18**, 4 (2015)
15. Caram, L.F., Caiafa, C.F., Ausloos, M., Proto, A.N.: Cooperative peer-to-peer multiagent-based systems. Phys. Rev. E **92**, 022805 (2015)
16. Braithwaite, D.W., Goldstone, R.L.: Effects of variation and prior knowledge on abstract concept learning. Cogn. Instr. **33**, 226–256 (2015)

Modeling the Behaviour of Economic Agents as a Response to Information on Tax Audits

Suriya Kumacheva[1]([✉])(iD), Elena Gubar[1](iD), Ekaterina Zhitkova[1](iD), and Galina Tomilina[2](iD)

[1] Faculty of Applied Mathematics and Control Processes, St. Petersburg State University, Universitetskii prospekt 35, Petergof, Saint-Petersburg 198504, Russia
{s.kumacheva,e.gubar,e.zhitkova}@spbu.ru
[2] EPAM Systems, Inc., Pevchesky per., 12, Saint-Petersburg 197101, Russia
g.tomilina@yandex.ru
http://www.spbu.ru

Abstract. Information is a strategic tool in many areas of the economics, business and social processes. Particularly, information can be considered as a control action in the problem of tax control. Following recent studies, we consider the auditing probabilities, which guarantee the absence of tax deviations, as the optimal strategies of the tax authority, however an employment of this strategy is unprofitable for tax authority and thus practically impossible. Therefore the dissemination of information on future tax audits over the taxable population can be offered as one of specific methods to stimulate people to pay taxes. Previously, it has been proofed that the process of information spreading resembles evolutionary dynamics in nature. Therefore, we consider a set of taxpayers as a population of interacted economic agents which intercommunicate with information/rumors. We design the propagation process as an imitation evolutionary dynamics over the structured population. We assume that it is more natural that agents will spread information or rumors over their own contact network, including neighbors and colleagues instead of randomly chosen agents. Thus in current study we investigate the imitation dynamics over the networks with different topology. We consider series of experiments where information spreads in the network of taxpayers with different topology and different modifications of bimatrix games to construct evolutionary dynamics describing the changes of agents behaviour. Numerical simulations give visualization of the information dissemination process over the different variant of the networks, imitation protocols and players payoffs. The results of simulations confirmed the influence of information on the final distribution of tax payments among the population with different levels of the risk propensity.

Keywords: Tax evasions · Tax control · Information dissemination · Evolutionary game · Networks

© Springer Nature Switzerland AG 2019
N. Agarwal et al. (Eds.): MSBC 2019, CCIS 1079, pp. 96–111, 2019.
https://doi.org/10.1007/978-3-030-29862-3_8

1   Introduction

In the modern world, an access to information helps people to make a decision about her/his strategy and choose an action which leads to success. The current study investigates such important problem as the impact of the information on possible tax audits on individuals' decisions to evade taxation or not [1,2]. Earlier in [8–10,16] based on the static model [4] we have constructed a dynamic system to describe the process of dissemination of information over the network of taxpayers. In the current study we use this system as the basic model to present the problem of taxation in a large but finite population of taxpayers.

In a series of papers on tax modeling [4,5,23], the conclusion about optimal tax control strategies was formulated as a "threshold rule". Numerical implementation of such strategies is an expensive procedure. In practice, it can be considered as unattainable due to the limited state budget. Therefore the tax authority needs to look for additional ways of encouraging taxpayers to fair tax payments. Among such incentives the dissemination of information about future audits can be considered as a useful tool. For example, an information can be similar to that the real probability is at least equal to the optimal probability value according to the mentioned "threshold rule", and be spread among the taxpayers, further mentioned as economic agents.

During the past decades different models for the propagation viruses and information in networks have been developed. One of the first papers, applying epidemic processes to the spreading of the rumors, ideas and information, is [7]. In many sources such as [12,17] information is considered as "infection of the mind" and its spreading can be formulated as epidemic or evolutionary process.

In the current paper we formulate a model of spreading information as an evolutionary network game to analyze how the dissemination of information affects on the decision of agents to evade taxation or not. Additionally, not only information, but also many other factors such as topology of the contact network, conflicts between agents etc. can also influence this decision.

In contrast to previous studies [20,24], where exampled agents were chosen at random, in the presented work construction of evolutionary dynamics of imitation is based on usage of special algorithms of choosing neighbors. Moreover, bimatrix games with different structure underlie the definition of the dynamics. Along with models built for risk-neutral agents [8–10,14], in the current study we also consider population, where agents with a different propensity to risk can change their actions, depending on external circumstances, as it was done in [15]. Due to this fact we design various scenarios of taxpayers' behaviour.

As we have showed in the previous researches [8,9,16] it is natural to represent a population of taxpayers as a connected network, because usually people prefer to share information with their family, neighbors, colleagues and friends. Following this assumptions we run the series of numerical experiments over the networks with different topology.

The paper is organized as follows. In Sect. 1, we present the overview of the basic and dynamic models. Section 2 presents the models of behaviour of risk-neutral agents in Subsect. 2.1 and the reaction of the system in the model for agents with different risk propensity in Subsect. 2.2 . In Sect. 3, we present the network model of annual process of tax audit. In Sect. 4, we present numerical simulation to illustrate the results. The paper is concluded in Sect. 5.

2   Aggregated System Costs in the Basic Models

In this paragraph we will obtain aggregated system costs for the cases of the model considered as a basis for dynamic processes of the information spreading.

2.1   Model with Risk-Neutral Agents

This section presents the problem of tax control based on the static model [4]. Due to the mentioned work we consider a large but finite population of n tax-payers, where ξ is true income, η is declared income, $\eta \leq \xi$. In the current model, $\xi, \eta \in \{L, H\}$, where $0 < L < H$, similar to [3]. Therefore here we obtain two groups of population: n_H and n_L, where

$$n_L + n_H = n.$$

Let P_L be the probability of random audit of agents, who declared income $\eta = L$. In the case when the tax arrears is revealed, the evader should pay $(\theta + \pi)(\xi - \eta)$, where constants θ and π are tax and penalty rates correspondingly.

For every profile of tax paying we obtain three possible taxpayers' profit functions:

$$u\left(L(L)\right) = (1 - \theta) \cdot L; \tag{1}$$

$$u\left(H(H)\right) = (1 - \theta) \cdot H; \tag{2}$$

$$u\left(L(H)\right) = H - \theta L - P_L(\theta + \pi)(H - L). \tag{3}$$

According to the "Threshold rule" obtained in [4,5,23] risk-neutral taxpayers refuse their evasion from H to L levels of income if probability P_L satisfies the condition

$$P_L \geq P^* = \frac{\theta}{\theta + \pi}. \tag{4}$$

Due to the limited budget of the tax authority, the optimal values of auditing probabilities P^* are extremely rare reached in real life. Therefore the tax author-ity needs to find additional methods to stimulate taxpayers to be honest. As one of these ways the dissemination of information about increased probability of tax auditing in the population of taxpayers can be considered. In particular, this information can take the form of a message "$P_L \geq P^*$". It means that dis-seminated information contains the statement that the share of the taxpayers randomly selected for auditing will be at least equal to the value P^* which is critical for the agents' decision to evade or not.

Construction of the model of information spreading needs some additional statements:

- The first statement is that the considered population is the set of size n_H, which consists only of the taxpayers with high level H of income. Therefore we suppose that in the case when there is no information the total population evades. Thus we can denote the number of evaders as n_{ev} and determine it in this case as $n_{ev} = n_H$.
- When information has been injected at the initial time moment in the population then the number of taxpayers informed about increased probability of tax auditing becomes $n_{inf}^0 = n_{nev}^0$. These agents are informed directly and therefore they decided not to evade. In each time moment $n_H = n_{ev}(t) + n_{nev}(t)$ (or $\nu_{nev}(t) + \nu_{ev}(t) = 1$, where ν_{nev}, ν_{ev} are the shares of evaders and non-evaders correspondingly), $t \in [0, T]$.

Moreover, at the initial time moment, the expected income of tax authority can be defined as the total tax revenue TTR_0^N in the absence of information, which includes only payments of agents with true income level L:

$$TTR_0^N = n_L \theta L + n_H \left(\theta\, L + P_L\, (\theta + \pi)(H - L) \right) - n\, P_L\, c, \tag{5}$$

where c is the unit cost of auditing.

At the final time moment T the total tax revenue TTR_T^N is computed in the assumption that the information was spread and the system has come to a steady state:

$$TTR_T^N = n_L \theta L + n_H \left(\nu_{nev}^T \theta H + \nu_{ev}^T \left(\theta L + P_L(\theta + \pi)(H - L) \right) \right) \\ - n(P_L\, c + \nu_{inf}^0 c_{inf}), \tag{6}$$

where ν_{nev}^T is the share of honest taxpayers, who do not evade at the moment $t = T$, ν_{ev}^T is the share of agents, who continue to evade taxation at the moment $t = T$, ν_{inf}^0 is the value (fraction) of the informational injection at the initial time moment $(\nu_{inf}^0 = \nu_{inf}(t_0))$ and c_{inf} is the unit cost of such injection, it is assumed that $c_{inf} << c$.

2.2   Model with Agents with Different Risk-Propensity

However, the real life brings more interesting effects to the interactions between tax authority and taxpayers. Thus, in considered population there can exist individuals with different risk-propensity: risk-averse, risk-neutral and risk-loving. It means that total population of taxpayers should be divided into three subgroups, as it was supposed in [15]. These subgroups differ from each other by the various agents' behaviour profiles in the similar external conditions. Therefore their response on the same information should be different. At the initial time moment in the absence of information only taxpayers with low level of income and risk avoiding agents (whose share is ν_a) pay. It means that in this case the total tax revenue is

$$TTR_0^R = n_L \theta L + n_H \left(\nu_a \theta H + (1 - \nu_a) P_L(\theta + \pi)(H - L) \right) - n P_L\, c. \tag{7}$$

At the final moment T when the information was spread and the system has come to a steady state the total tax revenue TTR_T^R is

$$TTR_T^R = n_L \theta L + n_H \left(\nu_a \theta H + (1 - \nu_a)(\nu_{nev}^T \theta H + \nu_{ev}^T(\theta L + P_L(\theta + \pi)(H - L)))) \right) \\ - n(P_L c + \nu_{inf}^0 c_{inf}).$$

(8)

3   Network Model

In this paragraph we formulate some basic assumptions of the network evolutionary model. Generally, in evolutionary game, a population of agents, who possess different types of behaviour, is divided into several subpopulations, in compliance with a number of types of behaviors. In the entire population pairwise interactions are defined by the bimatrix games, which describe all possible communications between randomly matching players. In contrast to original formulation of the evolutionary game, where evolution of the population is described through the set of random meetings in the well mixed population, we suppose that the social connection of each agents or taxpayer can be represented by the networks with different topology. Therefore, the interagent interactions are feasible only between connected taxpayers. Hence the evolution process differs from the ordinary evolutionary game. Following [8,20] we consider the process of disseminating information about inspections in the taxpayers' network as an evolutionary process in the population of economic agents. We design the algorithms of propagation based on the imitation rules [21,24]. In the current paper we consider three algorithms for selecting neighbors as an exampled agent in the imitation dynamics. The first one is random choice: an opponent agent is randomly selected from a set of agents who connected with the active agent. The second is based on the most influential neighbor: the opponent with the most direct connections to other agents is selected from the set of neighboring agents. If there are several agents with an equally large number of links, the choice between them is random. The third one is based on the neighbor with the highest income: an exampled neighbor is selected if his/her income, according to the results of the first iteration step, was the greatest.

3.1   Instant Games

In this subsection we consider a structured population of economic agents (taxpayers). As in [21,24] the instant communications between taxpayers is defined by two-players symmetric bimatrix game $\Gamma(A, B)$. Every taxpayer can choose one of two behaviors $X = \{ev, nev\}$, where ev is the behaviour "not evade", nev is the behaviour "to evade". Payoff matrix of the instant game between connected agents has structure of one of the following classical games: the Prisoner's Dilemma, the Stag Hunt game, the Hawk-Dove game. Since the structure of these bimatrix games is well-known then they are appropriated to estimate an impact of network structure and imitation rules. Further, an instant interaction can be modelled by using special structure of the game.

However we use the modification of Prisoner's Dilemma game [19], which can be described by the bimatrix game, presented below, where a payoff matrix of the first player is A and payoff matrix of the second player is symmetric $B = A^T$ [24]:

	C	D
C	$(\bar{u}+SW),(\bar{u}+SW)$	$(\bar{u}-SW, u(L(H)))$
D	$(u(L(H)),\bar{u}-SW)$	$(\bar{u},\bar{u})$

where C is the strategy "to cooperate", which can be interpreted "to pay taxes" in our case, D is the strategy "to defeat" which is equal to "to evade" in the studied model, $\bar{u} = 1/2u(L(L))+1/2u(H(H))$ is the average profit of the "mean" agent, SW is social welfare, obtained for the participation in social consolidation. The payoff matrix describes possible meetings between two honest taxpayers with strategies C, two evaders, who use strategies D, as well as two asymmetric situation profiles define interactions between honest taxpayer and evader. Hereafter in the next two games we follow the same technique.

In the Stag Hunt game [22] a payoff matrices A and $B = A^T$ are formed in the following way:

	S	I
S	$(\bar{u}+SW,\bar{u}+SW)$	$(0,\bar{u}-SW)$
I	$(\bar{u}-SW,0)$	$(\bar{u}-SW,\bar{u}-SW)$

where strategy S corresponds to social strategy "to hunt a stag" in classical form of the game, but in our case this strategy means to "to pay taxes", analogously strategy I corresponds to individual strategy "to hunt a hare" in original game, in our interpretation this a strategy recommends taxpayer "to evade".

The case of Hawk-Dove game is based on the payoff matrix A, $B = A^T$:

	F	D
F	$(\dfrac{u(L(H)) - (\theta+\pi)(H-L)}{2}, \dfrac{u(L(H)) - (\theta+\pi)(H-L)}{2})$	$(\bar{u}+SW,0)$
D	$(0,\bar{u}+SW)$	$(\dfrac{\bar{u}+SW}{2}, \dfrac{\bar{u}+SW}{2})$

where strategy F originally corresponds "to be a Hawk", which means that agent demonstrates an aggressive behaviour, in our case this strategy leads taxpayer "to evade", strategy D is "to be a Dove" and forces agent to follow a passive behaviour, in our case this behaviour is "to pay taxes". Additionally, we assume that the condition $u(L(H)) << (\theta+\pi)(H-L)$ should be satisfied and it works for the large values of the parameters θ and π or if the value of the difference $(H-L)$ is large.

3.2   Imitation Rules on the Networks

As it was mentioned above in the Sect. 3 an evolutionary process occurs on the indirect network $G = (N, K)$, where $N = \{1, \ldots, n_H\}$ is a set of economic agents and $K \subset N \times N$ is an edge set (each edge in K represents two-players symmetric game between connected taxpayers) [8,20]. It is assumed that the taxpayers choose strategies from a binary set $X = \{ev, nev\}$ and receive payoffs according to the matrix of payoffs. Each instant time moment agents use a single strategy against all opponents and thus the games occurs simultaneously. The strategy state: $x(T) = (x_1(t), \ldots, x_{n_H}(t))^T$, where $x_i(t) \in X$ is a strategy of taxpayer i, $i = \overline{1, n_H}$, at time moment t. Aggregated payoff of agent i will be defined as in [20]:

$$u_i = \omega_i \sum_{j \in M_i} a_{x_i(t), x_j(t)}, \tag{9}$$

where $a_{x_i(t), x_j(t)}$ is a component of payoff matrix, $M_i := \{j \in L : \{i, j\} \in K\}$ is a set of neighbors for taxpayer i, weighted coefficient $\omega_i = 1$ for cumulative payoffs and $\omega_i = \frac{1}{|M_i|}$ for average payoffs. Vector of payoffs of the total population is $u(t) = (u_1(t), \ldots, u_{n_H}(t))^T$.

The state of population will be changed according to the rule, which is a function of the strategies and payoffs of neighboring agents:

$$x_i(t + i) = f(\{x_j(t), u_j(t) : j \in N_i \cup \{i\}\}). \tag{10}$$

This rule dictates a method of imitation or adaptation of agents to the changes in his/her environment, which means that taxpayer can change her behaviour if at least one neighbor has the better payoff. As an example of such dynamics we can use the proportional imitation rule [21,24], in which each agent chooses a neighbor randomly and if this neighbor received a higher payoff by using a different strategy, then the agent will switch with a probability proportional to the payoff difference. The proportional imitation rule can be presented as:

$$p\left(x_i(t + 1) = x_j(t)\right) := \left[\frac{\lambda}{|M_i|} (u_j(t) - u_i(t)) \right]_0^1 \tag{11}$$

for each agent $i \in K$ where $j \in M_i$ is a uniformly randomly chosen neighbor, $\lambda > 0$ is an arbitrary rate constant, and the notation $[z]_0^1$ indicates $\max(0, \min(1, z))$.

In our work, we define three modifications of imitation rules, in compliance with the method of choice an exampled agent, taxpayers' payoffs and distribution of risk-statuses of taxpayers over the entire population. The main assumption of the work is the application of these imitation rules only to the subgroup of risk-neutral taxpayers, as far as, in our hypothesis, this group is the most influenceable on the tax collections in the entire population. Fractions of risk-loving and risk-averse taxpayers are fixed at the initial time moment.

- **Rule 1.** *Random neighbor.* When a taxpayer i receives an opportunity to revise her strategy then she chooses an exampled agent at random with equal probability to all connected neighbors.

- **Rule 2.** *Neighbor with the highest payoff.* When agent i receives an opportunity to revise her strategy then she considers current payoffs of all taxpayers and chooses an agent (or a set of agents) with maximum payoff. If there are several agents with maximum payoff then an exampled agent is chosen at random between this subset.
- **Rule 3.** *The most influenceable neighbor.* Firstly, taxpayer i estimates a number of connections of all nearest neighbors and selects an exampled agent from the set of agents with the maximum number of links. If there are several agents with maximum links, then an opponent is selected at each iteration of the dynamic process at random between the subset of influenceable agents.

4 Numerical Simulations

In current section we present numerical simulations which illustrate the theoretical approach described above. As the initial distribution of the population's propensity to risk, Gaussian distribution quantiles or curves obtained in the works [6, 11] can be considered. In the current study, to conduct numerical simulations we use the following results of psychological research on risk-addiction [18]: the number of risk-loving agents from the general population of taxpayers is 18%, risk-neutral agents are 65%, risk-avoidants are 17%. In all experiments we work with the distribution of the income among the population of Russian Federation in 2018 [25]. According to the model we consider only two levels of income are accessible for each taxpayer: low and high (L and H). After the unification of groups with different levels of income according to the economic reasons, we calculate the average levels of income L and H (the mathematical expectations of the uniform and Pareto distributions [13]) and receive the corresponding shares of the population (see Table 1).

Table 1. Two modeled groups and average income

Group	Income interval (rub./month)	Average income (rub.)	Share of population (%)
L	Less 25000	$L = 12500$	51
H	More 25000	$H = 50000$	49

For all experiments we fix the values of parameters: $\nu_a = 17\%$ is a share of risk-averse taxpayers in population, tax rate is $\theta = 13\%$, penalty rate is $\pi = 13\%$, optimal value of the probability of audit is $P^* = 0.5$, actual value of the probability of audit for those who declared L is $P_L = 0.1$, unit cost of auditing is $c = 7455$ (rub.), as a unit cost of information injection we consider $c_{inf} = 10\%c = 745.5$ (rub.).

The matrixes of the following games are used as scoring matrices: the Prisoner's Dilemma, the Stag Hunt game, the Hawk-Dove game. Each agent evaluates his profit using these matrices and information about the strategies of the

neighboring agents, with whom he has connections. Two algorithms for calculating this rating are considered:

- Cumulative: the sum of the profits from each interaction is computed;
- Average: the sum of the profits from interactions divided by their number.

If we take for $x_i(t)$ the i-th agent' profit at iteration t, then the $(t+1)$-th
iteration can be considered as final if: $\sqrt{\sum_{i=1}^{n}(x_i(t) - x_i(t+1))} \leq 3 \cdot 10^{-2}$.

The experiment for the same initial distribution was repeated a 10^2 times,
after which a report was generated.

Three examples below present different combination of instant games, protocols and method of computing of total tax revenue. In all examples initial
distribution of evaders and honest taxpayers is the same: $\nu_{ev}^0 = 13$, $\nu_{nev}^0 = 12$,
and the size of total population is $N = 25$. This size of population have been
chosen to simplify perception of the figures. The created software product allows
carrying out similar experiments for a population of larger sizes. However, the
conclusions obtained from these experiments are hampered by a sharply increasing number of cases that need to be analyzed.

Figures 1–2, 4–5 and 7–8 demonstrate the evolution of the shares of taxable
population during the iteration process. We use the following notation:

- agents with strategy "to pay taxes" are drown by squares, agents who use
  strategy "to evade" are drown by circles respectively;
- the risk status of agents is displayed by using the colors in the figures: risk-
  averse taxpayers are green nodes, risk-neutrals are red and risk-loving are
  blue.

To present the dynamic process in the population we use following modification of the network:

- strongly connected network, where the probability of link formation is $1/10$;
- weakly connected network, where the probability of link formation is $1/3$;
- random graph, where the probability of link formation is $1/k, k \in N$.

Example 1. In this example the following combination of parameters has used:
graph is grid, instant game is Prisoner's Dilemma and imitation rule is the most
influenceable neighbor. The pictures 1–2 present initial and final states of the
system subject to cumulative method of computing of agent's profit.

Series of numerical experiments have produced a set of data for estimation
of the influence of various parameters on the level of TTR^R. Some series of
experiments present the dependence of the total tax revenue on the number of
agents who chose the strategy "to pay". Experiments for the cumulative profit
of the dynamics of TTR^R, which depends on the share of honest taxpayers,
demonstrate more stable results and hence we use these examples as more illus-
trative. Below in Fig. 3 the mentioned dynamics are presented for the series of
experiments with the cumulative type of payoff.

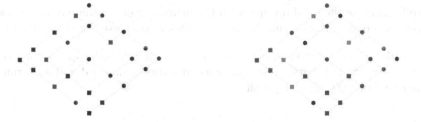

Fig. 1. Experiment I. Initial state of the population is $\nu_{ev}^0 = 13$, $\nu_{nev}^0 = 12$, initial total tax revenue is $TTR_0^R = 52082.86$;

Fig. 2. Experiment I. Final state of the population is $\nu_{ev}^T = 15$, $\nu_{nev}^T = 10$, method of computing of agent's profit: cumulative, final total tax revenue $TTR_T^R = 65210.50$.

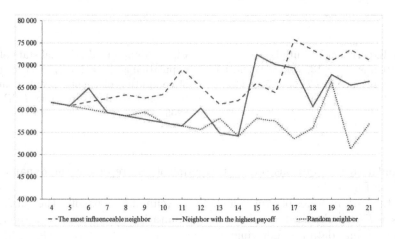

Fig. 3. Experiment Series I. The dynamics of TTR^R depending on the number of agents who pay. The ordinate axis represents the values of TTR^R, and the abscissa axis shows the number of honest taxpayers.

In Example 1 we have series of experiments for the cumulative payoffs, where the maximum values of TTR_T^R obtained by using different imitation rules for the corresponding initial and final data are following:

- The most influenceable neighbor: $TTR_T^R = 75758.7$, initial state of the population is $\nu_{ev}^0 = 8, \nu_{nev}^0 = 17$; final state of population is $\nu_{ev}^T = 6, \nu_{nev}^T = 19$;
- Neighbor with the highest payoff: $TTR_T^R = 72490.78$, initial state of the population is $\nu_{ev}^0 = 10, \nu_{nev}^0 = 15$; final state of population is $\nu_{ev}^T = 9, \nu_{nev}^T = 16$;
- Random neighbor: $TTR_T^R = 66336.52$, initial state of the population is $\nu_{ev}^0 = 6, \nu_{nev}^0 = 19$; final state of population is $\nu_{ev}^T = 11, \nu_{nev}^T = 14$.

Dynamics of the total revenue demonstrate different behavior, for example, imitation rules "the most influenceable neighbor" and "neighbor with the highest payoff" increase the total revenue with the increasing of the share of honest tax-payers, whereas imitation rule "random neighbor" decrease the value of TTR^R.

Example 2. The next example presents results of simulations for strong connected network with "Stag hunt" game as an instant game and imitation rule is "the neighbor with highest payoff".

Fig. 4. Experiment II. Initial state of the population is $\nu_{ev}^0 = 13, \nu_{nev}^0 = 12$, initial total tax revenue is $TTR_0^R = 52082.86$;

Fig. 5. Experiment II. Final state of the population is $\nu_{ev}^T = 4, \nu_{nev}^T = 21$, method of computing of agent's profit: cumulative, final total tax revenue $TTR_T^R = 82657.93$.

Similar to the previous series of experiment, we represent the dynamics of TTR^R in Fig. 6.

In the current series of experiments for the cumulative payoffs, the maximum values of TTR_T^R obtained by using different imitation rules for the corresponding initial and final data are following:

- The most influenceable neighbor: $TTR_T^R = 83403.43$, initial state of the population is $\nu_{ev}^0 = 14, \nu_{nev}^0 = 11$; final state of population is $\nu_{ev}^T = 4, \nu_{nev}^T = 21$;
- Neighbor with the highest payoff: $TTR_T^R = 84894.43$, initial state of the population is $\nu_{ev}^0 = 16, \nu_{nev}^0 = 9$; final state of population is $\nu_{ev}^T = 4, \nu_{nev}^T = 21$;
- Random neighbor: $TTR_T^R = 85639.93$, initial state of the population is $\nu_{ev}^0 = 17, \nu_{nev}^0 = 8$; final state of population is $\nu_{ev}^T = 4, \nu_{nev}^T = 21$.

The second example presents a very interesting dynamics of TTR^R, from the initial share of non-evaders to $\nu_{nev} = 7, \ldots, 9$ the value of total revenue archives its peaks and then decreases. However the general trend is the increasing of total tax revenue for all imitation rules.

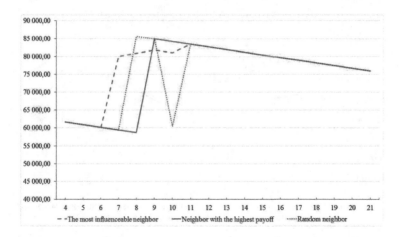

- -The most influenceable neighbor ——Neighbor with the highest payoff ·····Random neighbor

Fig. 6. Experiment Series II. The dynamics of TTR depending on the number of agents who pay. The ordinate axis represents the values of TTR^R, and the abscissa axis shows the number of honest taxpayers.

Example 3. The next example presents results of simulations for weakly connected network with "Hawk Dove" game as an instant game and imitation rule "random neighbor".

Fig. 7. Experiment III. Initial state of the population is $\nu_{ev}^0 = 13$, $\nu_{nev}^0 = 12$, initial total tax revenue is $TTR_0^R = 52082.86$;

Fig. 8. Experiment III. Final state of the population is $\nu_{ev}^T = 7$, $\nu_{nev}^T = 18$, method of computing of agent's profit: Cumulative, final total tax revenue $TTR_T^R = 77899.54$.

The dynamics of TTR^R on the number of non-evaders is represented in Fig. 9.

In the current series of experiments for the cumulative payoffs, the maximum values of TTR_T^R obtained by using different imitation rules for the corresponding initial and final data are following:

- The most influenceable neighbor: $TTR_T^R = 75948.43$, initial state of the population is $\nu_{ev}^0 = 4, \nu_{nev}^0 = 21$; final state of population is $\nu_{ev}^T = 4, \nu_{nev}^T = 21$;

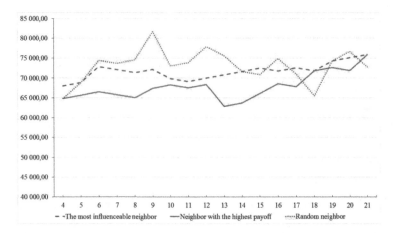

Fig. 9. Experiment Series III. The dynamics of TTR^R depending on the number of agents who pay. The ordinate axis represents the values of TTR^R, and the abscissa axis shows the number of honest taxpayers.

- Neighbor with the highest payoff: $TTR_T^R = 75948.43$, initial state of the population is $\nu_{ev}^0 = 4, \nu_{nev}^0 = 21$; final state of population is $\nu_{ev}^T = 4, \nu_{nev}^T = 21$;
- Random neighbor: $TTR_T^R = 81722.17$, initial state of the population is $\nu_{ev}^0 = 16, \nu_{nev}^0 = 9$; final state of population is $\nu_{ev}^T = 6, \nu_{nev}^T = 19$.

Here all dynamics fluctuate around mean value with weak tendency of increasing total revenue.

4.1   Experimental Results

By using the model of information spreading, we run 18 different cases of the initial distribution of risk statuses in the taxpayer population represented by networks with different configurations were considered in the series of numerical experiments. All experiments include grid, strongly connected and weakly connected random graphs. Evolutionary process of spreading information in the population of taxpayers is based on the bimatrix games such as "Prisoner's Dilemma", "Stag Hunt", "Hawks and Doves". For each initial distribution corresponding simulation was repeated 10^2 times to obtain statistically significant data to analyze the structure of possible scenarios. In addition, each experiments was performed for two types of payoffs: cumulative and average.

The series of experiments statistically demonstrate that regardless of network topology and the imitation rule, which is used for the Prisoner's Dilemma game, the strategy of evasion is stable. It is chosen by the majority of taxpayers in the most number of experiments.

At the same time, the game "Hawks and Doves" presents a completely opposite agents' behaviour: for any combination of imitations protocols, graphs and payoffs, agents prefer strategy "to pay". The results of the game "Stag Hunt" are generally similar to the results of the "Hawks and Doves" game. However, in the case of a weakly connected graph, we receive a tendency of the equiprobable (in a statistical sense) choice of both strategies by using "The Most Influential Neighbor" and "Neighbor with the highest payoff" imitation rules. The largest difference in the choice of strategies is demonstrated by the use of the Random Neighbor protocol.

It has also been revealed that the structure of the bimatrix game has the most influence on the final distribution of taxpayers. Regardless of the choice of imitation rules, the obtained results are completely comparable.

The most important result of numerical simulation is the ability to present the conclusions which type of network topology, imitation rules and type of bimatrix game improves the final attitude to the risk of the economic agents and, therefore, increases the level of declared income of taxpayers', in case of injected information circulates in the taxable population.

In addition, numerical simulations demonstrate two trends in changes of the total tax revenue of the system. Firstly, if the number of taxpayers, which pay taxes prevails over the number of evaders in the final distribution then a value of TTR_T^R increases in comparison with the initial total tax revenue TTR_R^0. Secondly, in some rare cases, total tax revenue grows even if a number of evaders is larger then a number of honest taxpayers in final distribution. This occurs because the collection of taxes and penalties increases, however, the probability of such event is small.

In some numerical experiments the dynamics of total tax revenue TTR_T^R have demonstrated unspecified results depending on the initial injection of information $\nu_{inf}^0 = \nu_{nev}^0$. For example, comparison of the results for different types of games or different topology of networks presents a tendency to decrease in total revenue TTR_T^R if the number of those who chose the strategy "to pay" increases. Whereas, analysis of the dynamics of TTR_T^R under various imitation rules, on the contrary, shows a tendency to increase the value of total tax revenue. Some simulations bring dynamics of TTR_T^R with large deviations from mean values of TTR_T^R. Hence, it is necessary to run additional series of experiments to receive more data sets to examine the trends more exact and that is the frame work for further research.

Comparison of the practical factors allows us to assess the efficiency of the proposed method of simulation the tax collection. This scenario analysis helps users to consider the process of information dissemination as a tool to improve the incentive and fiscal functions of the tax system. Additionally, the reduction of risk-loving agents helps to provide one of the fundamental principles of a tax system – the principle of fair taxation.

5   Conclusions

In the present work, the question of stimulating the taxable population to fair tax payments through the dissemination of information about future audits was studied.

The current study presents an impact of information dissemination about future audits over a taxable population to fair tax payments. This problem was formulated as the model, which combines ideas of applying the "Threshold rule" and evolutionary dynamics to imitating the actual information dissemination process. Moreover, evolutionary dynamics are considered not on the population of the randomly interacted agents but on the structured population which described by the network with different topology.

References

1. Antocia, A., Russua, P., Zarrib, L.: Tax evasion in a behaviorally heterogeneous society: an evolutionary analysis. Econ. Model. **10**(42), 106–115 (2014)
2. Antunes, L., Balsa, J., Urbano, P., Moniz, L., Roseta-Palma, C.: Tax compliance in a simulated heterogeneous multi-agent society. In: Sichman, J.S., Antunes, L. (eds.) MABS 2005. LNCS (LNAI), vol. 3891, pp. 147–161. Springer, Heidelberg (2006). https://doi.org/10.1007/11734680_11
3. Boure, V., Kumacheva, S.: A model of audit with using of statistical information about taxpayers' income. Vestnik SPbGU **10**(1–2), 140–145 (2005). (in Russian)
4. Boure, V., Kumacheva, S.: A game theory model of tax auditing using statistical information about taxpayers. Vestnik SPbGU **10**(4), 16–24 (2010). (in Russian)
5. Chander, P., Wilde, L.L.: A general characterization of optimal income tax enforcement. Rev. Econ. Studies **65**, 165–183 (1998)
6. Friedman, M., Savage, L.J.: The utility analysis of choices involving risk. J. Polit. Econ. **56**(4), 279–304 (1948)
7. Goffman, W., Newill, V.A.: Generalization of epidemic theory: an application to the transmission of ideas. Nature **204**(4955), 225–228 (1964)
8. Gubar, E., Kumacheva, S., Zhitkova, E., Kurnosykh, Z.: Evolutionary behavior of taxpayers in the model of information dissemination. In: Constructive Nonsmooth Analysis and Related Topics (Dedicated to the Memory of V.F. Demyanov, CNSA 2017) Proceedings, pp. 1–4. IEEE Conference Publications, St. Petersburg (2017)
9. Gubar, E., Kumacheva, S., Zhitkova, E., Kurnosykh, Z., Skovorodina, T.: Modelling of information spreading in the population of taxpayers: evolutionary approach. Contrib. Game Theory Manage. **10**, 100–128 (2017)
10. Gubar, E.A., Kumacheva, S.Sh., Zhitkova, E.M., Porokhnyavaya, O.Yu.: Propagation of information over the network of taxpayers in the model of tax auditing. In: 2015 International Conference on Stability and Control Processes in Memory of V.I. Zubov (SCP 2015) Proceedings, pp. 244–247. IEEE Conference Publications, St. Petersburg (2015)
11. Kahneman, D., Tversky, A.: Advances in prospect theory: cumulative representation of uncertainty. J. Risk Uncert. **5**, 297–323 (1992)
12. Kandhway, K., Kuri, J.: Optimal control of information epidemics modeled as Maki Thompson rumors. In: Preprint submitted to Communications in Nonlinear Science and Numerical Simulation (2014)
13. Kendall, M.G.: A. Stuart, Distribution Theory, Nauka, Moscow (1966). (in Russian)
14. Kumacheva, S.S.: Tax auditing using statistical information about taxpayers. Contrib. Game Theory Manage. **5**, 156–167 (2012)
15. Kumacheva, S.S., Gubar, E.A.: Evolutionary model of tax auditing. Contrib. Game Theory Manage. **8**, 164–175 (2015)

16. Kumacheva, S., Gubar, E., Zhitkova, E., Tomilina, G.: Evolution of risk-statuses in one model of tax control. In: Petrosyan, L., Mazalov, V., Zenkevich, N. (eds.) Frontiers of Dynamic Games. Static and Dynamic Game Theory: Foundations and Applications, pp. 121–138. Birkhauser, Cham (2018)
17. Nekovee, A.M., Moreno, Y., Bianconi, G., Marsili, M.: Theory of rumor spreading in complex social networks. Phys. A **374**, 457–470 (2007)
18. Niazashvili, A.: Individual differences in risk propensity in different social situations of personal development. Moscow University for the Humanities, Moscow (2007)
19. Owen, G.: Game Theory. Saunders Company, Philadelphia (1968)
20. Riehl, J.R., Cao M.: Control of stochastic evolutionary games on networks. In: 5th IFAC Workshop on Distributed Estimation and Control in Networked Systems, pp. 458–462. Philadelphia, PA, USA (2015)
21. Sandholm, W.H.: Population Games and Evolutionary Dynamics. The M.I.T. Press, Cambridge (2010)
22. Skyrms, B.: The Stag Hunt and the Evolution of Social Structure. Cambridge University Press, Cambridge (2003)
23. Vasin, A., Morozov, V.: The Game Theory and Models of Mathematical Economics. MAKS Press, Moscow (2005). (in Russian)
24. Weibull, J.: Evolutionary Game Theory. The M.I.T. Press, Cambridge (1995)
25. The web-site of the Russian Federation State Statistics Service. http://www.gks.ru/

Behaviour Patterns in Expert Recognition by Means of Structured Expert Judgement in Price Estimation in Customized Furniture Manufacturing

Birutė Mikulskienė[✉], Viktor Medvedev, Tomas Vedlūga, and Olga Navickienė

Mykolas Romeris University, Ateities str. 20, 08303 Vilnius, Lithuania
birute.mikulskiene@mruni.eu

Abstract. The furniture manufacturing sector of the Baltics is facing serious challenges common in all European countries, namely, the growing global competition for customized solutions. New standards to be followed in the industry tend to increase production costs, extend manufacturing time and cause frequent errors in the product quality. To maintain sustainability, companies need decision support instruments, allowing an immediate reaction to customized orders and proper evaluation of manufacturing procedures, costs and deadlines. The complex problem of cost estimation at an early stage could be solved partly by strengthening operational research in decision support systems supplemented with machine learning techniques. Additional reliability could be acquired complementing an intelligent system with a human knowledge intervention and applying outcomes of behavioural operational research. Scientific and methodological issues of how to integrate the output of structured expert judgement into an intelligent cost estimation system is a pressing problem. The goal of the present research is to look into the cultural pattern of competence recognition within furniture industry with the purpose to adjust the structural expert judgement strategy as an instrument to validate expert input into the decision support tool for cost estimation. The research is based on mix method strategy (a qualitative study, a quantitative study and a structured expert judgement experiment). The findings clearly highlighted that a well-composed group of experts could be a possible solution in assessing uncertain aspects of cost estimation. Although the cultural model of the furniture sector would recommend a slightly different approach: the top executives and the best engineers in this sector are seen as experts. This should be taken into account when developing methodological recommendations for the implementation of the structured expert judgement.

Keywords: Behavioural operational research · Structured expert judgement · Customize manufacturing · Cost estimation

N. Agarwal et al. (Eds.): MSBC 2019, CCIS 1079, pp. 112–125, 2019.
https://doi.org/10.1007/978-3-030-29862-3_9

1 Introduction

The furniture manufacturing sector of the Baltics is facing serious challenges common in all European countries, namely, the growing global competition for customized solutions [1]. New standards to be followed in the industry tend to increase production costs, extend manufacturing time and cause frequent errors in the product quality. To maintain sustainability, companies need decision support instruments, allowing an immediate reaction to customized orders and proper evaluation of manufacturing procedures, costs and deadlines. The task to estimate costs as precise as possible and as early as possible has become critically important in customized manufacturing. However, cost estimation at an early design stage makes a serious challenge for other sectors as well, e.g. nanotechnology, aircraft manufacturing, etc. [2]. New opportunities to deal with the problem may be suggested by newly emerging trends in extensive data research [3] and by operational research into decision support systems supplemented by machine learning techniques [4]. Complex decision making problems, as well as cost estimation problems, are often attributable to absence, insufficiency or inaccuracy of available data. Additional reliability could be acquired complementing an intelligent system with a human knowledge intervention and applying outcomes of behavioural operational research. In such cases, a structured expert judgement (SEJ) can be used. Therefore, it is worth discussing a meaningful use of expert knowledge to compensate the complexity of price calculation and foresee possible errors. Apart from scientific and methodological issues of how to integrate the output of structured expert judgement into an intelligent cost estimation system, there are additional questions to be tackled, e.g. expert recognition and building trust between the user of the decision support system and the expert. Thus, the complexity of cultural processes additionally enhances the complexity of customization.

The goal of the present research is to look into the cultural pattern of competence recognition within furniture industry with the purpose to adjust the structured expert judgement strategy as an instrument to validate expert input into the decision support tool for cost estimation.

The main question about a methodological recommendation for expert selection for SEJ is analysed in the frame of broader sectorial picture, e.g. (a) the pricing process, ICT usability and experts; (b) the accuracy of pricing forecasts by experts. The broader context of the research context has led to the choice of methods.

The paper is organised as follows. First, we are giving an overview of what is known about the widespread pricing methods then we are going to analyze how expert knowledge is applied in cost estimation and finally, we are going to discuss how to achieve a better integration of a particular strategy of structured expert judgement with a behavioural pattern adopted in customized manufacturing for the sake of price estimation. The research also reveals how to identify appropriate experts among the company's employees for further cost estimation.

2   Literature Review

Cost Estimation. Having screened the most common cost estimation techniques, one can find a simple and reliable method to estimate the cost by dividing a product into its constituent elements and estimating the cost on the basis of prices of individual components and time necessary to produce the element [5]. However, the simple technique based on adding up prices of individual components eventually turns into a complex task. The first moment for uncertainties to show up is when the choice between possible design solutions has to be made. Thus, the early design stage needs additional attention and reliable cost estimation procedures and models to be used [6]. A more comprehensive approach to the task of cost calculation is based on unbundling elements according to different levels of uncertainties. Three categories can be distinguished here: facts, estimated values and application parameters [5]. Facts are what is measured exactly at the end of the production process. Estimated values are the result of statistical observations or the data collected through experiments (e.g. working hours). Application parameters cover the part of the cost that comes up from different scenarios.

Customized manufacturing typically relies upon traditional cost estimation methods, most of which are based on the reaction to complexity. So far, attempts to estimate costs manually, especially at the early design stage, have failed to produce positive results due to the lack of accuracy, incompleteness of data and extensive consumption of time [7].

More and more sectors, including manufacturing, software engineering, process engineering, construction industry and scientific research, refer to instruments of artificial intelligence. Therefore, newly developed methods based on artificial intelligence and massive amounts of data have become a good opportunity for customized manufacturers. At the moment, the most popular analytical instruments include: analogous cost estimation, bottom-up estimation techniques, and computing technology combined with artificial intelligence.

Expert-Based Knowledge. Even with an application of various methods and multiple methodologies, the accuracy of cost estimation is still insufficient and is under question every time a new customized order is received. Also, because of tight deadlines, additional sources of knowledge must be sought in order to either correct or justify the preliminary numbers. A possible solution of the situation might be expert advice. Expert contribution is widely used in different areas "where an explicit conceptual framework does not exist or where data are very impoverished" [8]. Before addressing the question of how to deal with expert knowledge, we need to tackle the issue of expert recognition. There have been permanent debates about who may be referred to as an expert and how to select the best expert in the field. Recently, expert judgment has been increasingly recognized as another type of scientific data. Recognition of expert-based knowledge is almost inseparable from some cultural issues lying behind understanding the value added of professional knowledge. There is some tension between professional knowledge and any other knowledge, which could be represented by a complementary area or use of knowledge. In the meantime, there are more and more studies claiming that professional knowledge is more valuable than "practical wisdom of clients" [9]. It seems that these questions are still not answered completely, and there is some gap in the literature when product customization is discussed in terms of price estimation.

Although it has been recognized as an adequate source of additional knowledge for decision-making, expert knowledge is still difficult to integrate into a universal knowledge management system. Also, from the perspective of knowledge retention, different strategies to ensure knowledge accumulation are recognized. Knowledge retention can be implemented by maintaining three different approaches: technology-based, interaction-based (capturing the process and practices) and culture-based (best practices with interactions of professionals) [10]. The technology-based approach relies on collection and storage of information and factual data [11]. Interaction based knowledge accumulation means learning from previous mistakes and the culture-based approach means specialist expertise in a particular field [12]. Accuracy of pricing strongly depends on a chosen culture-based strategy that has direct links with practice and expert interaction. Culture based strategies differ between sectors depending on their size, nature, and other criteria. The choice is typically limited by formal skills of an expert and inclusion of other experts is understood as a cultural process, which is an integral part of price setting. The expert-based approach shall mostly consider the following: the complexity, dimensions and specifications of the furniture, the current market variables, the size of the market for specific furniture, the existence of risks in the market and the possible sales margin. However, the systematic process of selecting and using experts in price estimation is often ignored by businesses [12].

Structured Expert Judgment. Expert judgment includes a wide range of methods - from one opinion to think-tanks with external validation. Very often, parameters necessary for decision making or modeling physical or biological behaviour are not precisely known. Experts in different fields may have the necessary valuable knowledge of models and parameters applicable in their specific field of interest. Quantitative assessment and aggregation of expert opinions can provide an essential contribution to decision making and can lead to an optimal choice of model parameters. Expert opinions can be combined either by identifying them individually and explicitly and then applying some mathematical rule or by giving the group an opportunity to discuss problems and negotiate to agree on a consensus, what is also known as behavioural aggregation. Behavioural research has shown that a person's ability to encode judgments in probabilistic terms varies according to his experience [13]. There is some evidence that mathematical aggregation can outperform behavioural approaches [14].

Various mathematical methods can be practically used in combining expert judgement. Mathematical methods usually ensure that there is a common understanding of the questions among experts and the use of certain weights to combine expert assessments of uncertainties. The simplest method is to deem all the weights equal. Equal weight combinations have obvious advantages, however they have drawbacks as well. An expert whose distributions are very different from those given by other experts may have a significant impact on the resulting decision. This is a significant drawback if the expert assessments cannot be justified based on performance. As more and more experts are brought into the study, the equal weight decision maker can tend to become quiet diffuse [12]. Cooke's Classical approach [12, 15] which is known as structure expert judgement, is most frequently applied among all expert judgement methods.

Expert judgment is used in a wide range of areas, including nuclear safety [16, 17]; aircraft engineering [18]; air traffic control [19] and software production [20]. Expert judgement is also used extensively for cost estimation [21], where experts have to make assumptions and judgments about the cost of a new product. Expert judgment based estimation approaches are most commonly used in the software industry [20]. For example, the main procedural steps set in EXCALIBUR software are following [12, 22]: formation of an expert group, expert assessment of variables, identification of the true values, rating of experts in terms of calibration and informativeness, conversion of ratings into weights, questioning of experts about uncertainty of the results of possible measurements within their domain of expertise.

3   Methodology

To capture the cultural approach of the behaviour pattern towards expert recognition and to measure the accuracy of expert knowledge in the process of price estimation, a mix method research methodology has been chosen. The mix method strategy comprises three studies: a qualitative study, a quantitative study and an SEJ experiment. The qualitative study was conducted to find out what pricing stages are used by companies and how companies use expert knowledge to justify the accuracy of the price. This research has to provide the knowledge we need to invite the experts to the SEJ experiment and what kind of questions about prices are worth asking and what accuracy of price prediction we could expect. The quantitative survey was conducted with the aim of obtaining quantitative data on the use of expert knowledge for price calculation understanding the cultural pattern of competence recognition within furniture industry. The third study was an SEJ experiment during which expert elicitation and expert ability to predict the price were studied. The combination of the methods is expected to determine whether there are specific behavioural trends that could limit the application of SEJ in a furniture company. Another objective to be achieved is to investigate the possibility to adjust the structured expert judgement strategy as an instrument to validate expert input into the decision support tool for cost estimation.

Quality Study. The research was based on the semi-structural interview method. Two companies working in customized manufacturing were selected for the research. Data for the research were collected in the course of 26 interviews with a wide range of specialists within the company, including CEOs, managers, product developers, constructors. All interviews were transcribed and coded. The responses were grouped into categories and subcategories by means of the qualitative data analysis software NVivo. A total of 174 pages of text and 905 coded notions were grouped into four generalized categories: price estimation, the organizational structure, employee engagement and production processes. Having made the qualitative classification of statements into categories, a comparative analysis of the collected interview data was conducted to reveal fundamental similarities and differences between approaches of individual respondents. As the scale of the study was very large, only 1/5 of the data was used for the expert database. The present article analyses only the category of price estimation.

Quantitative Survey. The survey was conducted by an international market research company in the period from January to February 2019. 146 Lithuanian companies were interviewed as a sample representing furniture manufacturers. A set of 35 questions compiled specifically for the survey included five major factors of the conceptual model: the organizational structure, employee engagement, price estimation, production processes, and IT implementation. Although the overall research comprises a wide range of issues associated with customized furniture manufacturing, this particular survey focuses only on the part regarding price estimation and expert recognition. Here, questions about the structure of the organization, employee involvement in product pricing and employee assessment most typically taken into account are dealt with. The used 35-item questionnaire is reliable as the value of Cronbach's alpha coefficient is 0.809. The internal consistency of the 7-item list is also satisfactory for the Cronbach's alpha equal to 0.818.

Descriptive statistics and analysis of non-parametric statistics are used in the quantitative study. The Cochran's Q test is used to check existence of statistical differences between experts (company representative) opinions using their agreements as dichotomous variables. A null hypothesis that there would be no difference in percentages of agreements between the experts has been made and tested with the significance level of 0.01. In order to run Cochran's Q test, the study was designed so as to meet assumptions suggested by Sheskin [23]. A correlation analysis has been carried out to identify the strength of relationships between pairs of survey questions related to SEJ using Spearmen's Rank correlation coefficients with the significance level of 0.01. The relative strength of relationship between two question-items is based on interpretation of the relative strength of the significant Spearmen's correlation coefficients [24].

Structured Expert Judgement. The third part of the research is based on a structured approach to expert judgement [12, 15] in order to identify appropriate experts among the company's employees for further cost estimation. The composition of this group is an important issue. The survey was carried out in one of the Lithuanian furniture manufacturing companies. Ten employees (nominated as experts) took part in the research: a CEO, a constructor, a chief accountant, a chief financial officer, the head of the finance department, an IT manager, a designer, a senior project administrator, a project administrator and a chief product manager. The structured expert judgment involves two generic quantitative dimensions of expert performance: calibration and information. The calibration questionnaire included the following elements: general questions about the expert and seed questions. Each expert had to answer twenty seed questions about their experience, compiled for expert elicitation. Then, a list of several products was given for price estimation. Experts had to suggest possible prices on the basis of available data about the product, such as the materials, the quantity and the operational procedures. An EXCALIBUR software package [25] was used for structured expert judgement elicitation on the basis of Cooke's Classical Model [12], where two separate scores (calibration and information scores) are estimated and multiplied together to get the overall weight for each expert [26]. In order to estimate the scores, experts are given a set of seed questions. Experts were asked to submit their estimates with a certain tolerance, for example, minimum and maximum probable values, in other words, to specify quantiles of the distribution of interest, such as the 5th, 50th or 95th. The calibration and information scores combined together lead to a weight estimate for each expert [12, 15].

4 Findings

Qualitative research focused on the pricing process and its interfaces with engineering processes. After a detailed disclosure of the management stages of the price calculation, it becomes clearer what the issues of calibration and forecasting of SEJs are relevant to the furniture sector and their experts. The qualitative research has revealed an interesting approach to pricing and its importance in customized production. Pricing is a complex critical process crucial in customized production. The study has shown that it is extremely difficult to determine the exact price of a piece of furniture because it depends on a great deal of various factors. Each company uses different methods and methodologies of pricing. However, there are some general trends in modeling furniture prices. For example, some companies set prices after preparatory design works, while others rely upon immediately calculated average prices. Such differences affect the exact final price. Also, companies account for different factors when calculating their prices. Some pay more attention to the product design and the materials used, others focus primarily on the production time and the hourly cost of necessary operations. Bigger companies have departments responsible for price calculation. For example, a project department creates order and sends it to the pricing department. The pricing department calculates the costs and sends the numbers back to the project department where a certain mark-up is added. Smaller companies cannot afford having pricing department and therefore delegate the function to individual experts.

In terms of general trends in modeling furniture prices, analysis of price calculations comes up with two aspects of trends. The first aspect entails tangible and measurable product elements, such as product dimensions, production time, the number of produced units, the used materials and the market segment.

The other aspect is about intangible parameters that affect price calculation. Words like guesswork, collaboration, collective, meetings, intuition, client are typical here. The second trend is primarily predetermined by the influence of experts or experienced employees. It is the experts who are responsible for setting the product price. The study shows that most companies are looking for expert opinion, proposals or assistance in determining the final price of individualized furniture while experts admit that the process is based more on predictions and intuition rather than rationality. The main participants in pricing include senior managers, finance managers, engineer sand and even company directors.

The notion of "expert/experts" entails such concepts as self-determination, meetings, intuition, director's influence, independence, competence or qualification. The concepts are not only invoked to describe an expert but also are referred to by experts in price estimations.

The study clearly shows a certain conflict between the trends (aspects). Pricing is mostly determined by measurable criteria whereas expert judgment is largely about intangible elements difficult to measure. However, all the elements are equally important in pricing and no factor can be neglected as insignificant as each of the factors can have a significant impact on the final price of the product. All elements must be logically combined into a reasonable price expression.

Quantitative Survey – Cost/Price Estimation with a Limited Set of Professionals.
In Lithuanian furniture sector is dominated by small and medium-sized enterprises with only a few large companies employing more than 800 people. This determines their specific behaviour in dealing with pricing issues. 53% of the surveyed companies stated that the director is involved in the price calculation (14% among those claimed that the director is the only person responsible for pricing), 37% named the owner (10% – only the owner), 33% – the head of production department, 25% – the constructor, 24% – the designer and 17% – the project manager. In 37% of the companies, only one employee is involved in the calculation of prices: 14% – the director, 10% – the owner, 12% – other. 25% of the companies involve two employees, 17% – three employees, 13% – four, 5% – five, 3% – six employees. An interesting fact is that the majority of the companies have more than one employee responsible for pricing. Most companies recognize this stage of manufacturing as important and sensitive to the quality. That is why companies see the need to have an "advisor" to assist in the calculations.

Not surprisingly, opinions of only few delegated specialists are taken into consideration during the price estimation stage. In 20% of the surveyed companies, the director's proposals are the most important when pricing is discussed, in 16% it is the head of the production department and in 10% – the owner. 17% of the companies give major importance to proposals by the head's of the production department or another specialist (a project manager, a designer, a constructor or a technologist). Thus, a total of 33% of the companies tend to rely upon proposals by the head of the production department.

76% of the surveyed companies noted that only the director or the owner make the final decision on the price offered to the client. A further 11% of the respondents named the deputy director, the product manager, the project manager, an engineer designer or constructor as a co-maker of the final decision along with the director/owner. Thus, the owner or director has a say on the final decision on pricing in 87% of the companies. In 4% of the companies, the final decision on pricing is made by the product manager and in 2% – by the project manager. Practically in all surveyed furniture companies, prices are decided mostly by the director or other highly ranked manager delegated the power of decision.

To have a general idea about experiences and opinions about specialists (1) whose opinions are taken into account in the process of pricing, (2) who make final decisions on pricing, and (3) who have the greatest influence on the competitiveness of the product, a null hypothesis that there would be no difference in percentages of agreements between the experts has been made. The conducted Cochran's Q test maintained that there is no statistically significant difference in the proportion of expert opinions on the three question-points under consideration: (1) $\chi^2(145) = 168,458$, $p = 0,089$; (2) $\chi^2(145) = 62,969$, p = 1,000; (3) $\chi^2(145) = 145,087$, $p = 0,482$.

Companies mostly trust employees who contribute to competitiveness – designers, constructors and product managers. On the basis of calculations of the significant Spearmen rank-order correlation coefficients between pairs of questions about the level of the organizational structure, the professional status of the representative in the company; the rank of the specialist responsible for pricing, the rank of the specialist whose opinion is valued most and the rank of the specialist who makes the final decision on pricing, several assumptions can be made:

(1) The simpler the structure of the company is (e.g. all employees directly accountable to the head of the company), the higher professional status is required for pricing (e.g. the director or the owner) ($r_{s(144)} = -0.214$, $p = 0.01$).

(2) The higher position a company representative is holding, the more likely they are to take into account proposals of a senior employee ($r_{s(144)} = 0.250$, $p = 0.02$).

(3) The higher the qualification of a specialist in charge of pricing is, the more likely their price estimates are to be taken into account ($r_{s(144)} = 0.323$, $p = 0.07$).

SEJ. The previous research has shown that during the cost estimation process companies mostly trust such employees as designers, constructors and product managers. These findings, as well as obtained assumptions, were partially confirmed during the research based on a structured approach to expert judgement in order to identify appropriate experts among company's employees for further cost estimation. While recognition of the ability of top managers to predict prices has not been corroborated by SEJ results. It was noticed that a well-composed group of experts could be a possible resource in assessing uncertain aspects of cost estimation, as it has been observed in the quantitative survey.

Two sets of questions were prepared and used in the expert ranking experiment: (1) questions about the furniture sector, furniture economics and company demography and economics and (2) questions exceptionally about company economics and demography. The results of the expert judgment based on Cooke's classical model obtained by means of EXCALIBUR software (see Fig. 1) show that only two experts out of ten were found suitable as experts for further cost estimation, namely, the chief financial officer and the senior project administrator. An additional study was carried out having left only questions about internal processes in the company (11 seed questions) to rank the other experts. The results (see Fig. 2) show that the highest weights were given to the following experts: the IT manager and the chief product manager.

To achieve the goal of the research another experimental step was carried out to find out the possibility of using the structured expert judgement strategy for cost estimation in customized furniture manufacturing. Authentic data provided by a Lithuanian furniture manufacturing company were used in the survey. The data included the actual costs of the products. During the experiment, methods based on machine learning techniques were also used for cost estimation [27]. Six experts among company's employees took part in the experiment: the chief accountant, an IT manager, two designers, a project administrator and a chief product manager. Whereas the results of the quality study showed that pricing is mostly determined by measurable criteria, the costs were evaluated on the basis of the following data: the cost of materials, the list

Nr.	Id	Calibr.	Mean relative total	Mean relative realization	Numb real	UnNormalized weight	Normaliz.weigl without DM	Normaliz.weig with DM
1	ZG	1,022E-008	1,724	1,724	19	0	0	0
2	LA	3,139E-011	1,449	1,449	20	0	0	0
3	DM	7,213E-010	1,896	1,896	20	0	0	0
4	NA	1,215E-007	1,165	1,165	20	0	0	0
5	MG	1,673E-005	1,336	1,336	20	2,236E-005	0,3489	0,0006074
6	MK	2,099E-007	1,714	1,714	20	0	0	0
7	DB	3,134E-007	1,405	1,405	19	0	0	0
8	LG	8,33E-013	2,049	2,049	20	0	0	0
9	VK	2,534E-005	1,646	1,646	20	4,172E-005	0,6511	0,001133
10	JM	2,506E-009	1,696	1,696	20	0	0	0

Fig. 1. Results of scoring experts (20 seed questions, global weights).

Nr.	Id	Calibr.	Mean relative total	Mean relative realization	Numb real	UnNormalized weight	Normaliz.weigl without DM	Normaliz.weig with DM
1	ZG	0,002841	1,549	1,549	11	0	0	0
2	LA	3,651E-005	1,719	1,719	11	0	0	0
3	DM	2,614E-006	1,322	1,322	11	0	0	0
4	NA	0,002126	1,024	1,024	11	0	0	0
5	MG	0,01364	1,538	1,538	11	0	0	0
6	MK	0,01811	1,223	1,223	11	0,02216	0,3178	0,03204
7	DB	9,874E-005	1,097	1,097	10	0	0	0
8	LG	3,82E-005	1,73	1,73	11	0	0	0
9	VK	0,037	1,286	1,286	11	0,04756	0,6822	0,06879
10	JM	8,967E-006	1,192	1,192	11	0	0	0

Fig. 2. Results of scoring experts (11 seed questions, equal weights).

and duration of the manufacturing procedures. The obtained results are presented in Fig. 3. Expert No. 1 (the chief accountant), Expert No. 2 (the IT manager) and Expert No. 5 (the chief product manager) were identified as the most appropriate in the previous study. The results show that the cost estimation given by Expert No. 1 (the chief accountant) is very close to the actual price of the product and the cost obtained by machine learning-based techniques. However, in order to use machine learning techniques, it is crucial to have a proper set of historical data for the training process and to identify essential data features to obtain accurate results. Meanwhile, experts can make cost estimates in the absence of historical data.

To sum up, a well-composed group of experts can be a possible solution in assessing uncertain aspects of cost estimation. The composition of such a group is an important issue. The general requirement for the experts is that the group needs to have some specific knowledge necessary to understand the technical, organizational and financial side of the cost estimation. Apart from hiring expert team members, who have the necessary knowledge, is also advisable to refer to the necessary external experts for alternative opinions. Also, it has to be noted that essential insights and valuable opinions may come from individuals who cannot be immediately identified as experts [28].

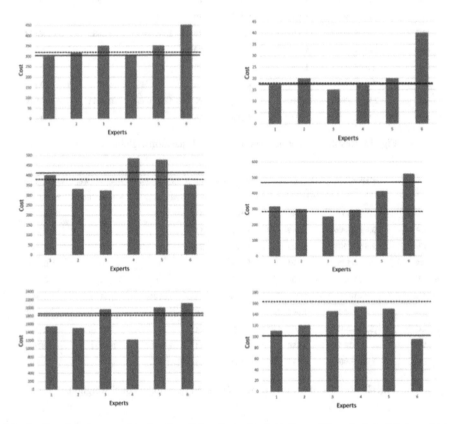

Fig. 3. Results of cost estimation for six products (straight line – the real cost of the product, dotted line – machine learning-based cost estimation)

5   Conclusions

The main intention of this study was to investigate whether there are behavioural patterns within the particular sector that limits smooth integration of different methods (machine learning and expert judgment) during operational decision (cost estimation) task.

Price estimation at the early design stage not only gives an opportunity for optimization of costs but also positively contributes to the development of customized production processes. The survey in the principles that companies would expect from a Custom Order Price Estimation System has come up with strong arguments in favour of material-based pricing systems, whereas systems based on ex-peer evaluations are subject to criticism. Analysis of how companies rely on experts has revealed several trends. Pricing in furniture industry is the prerogative of several professionals who are responsible for setting the right price. This was confirmed by both the quantitative survey and a qualitative interview. The trend has also been confirmed by means of an SEJ experiment. Selected experts among company's employees demonstrate better results both in expert rating and price forecasting. Meanwhile, recognition of the ability of top managers to predict prices has not been corroborated by SEJ results. The fact might reflect both a limited distribution of responsibilities and a clear division of management responsibilities.

It was noticed in the research that a well-composed group of experts could be a possible solution in assessing uncertain aspects of cost estimation. The general requirement for the experts is that the group needs to have some specific knowledge necessary to understand the technical, organizational and financial side of the cost estimation. Although the cultural model of the furniture sector would recommend a slightly different approach: the top executives and the best engineers in this sector are seen as experts. This should be taken into account when developing methodological recommendations for the implementation of the structured expert judgement.

Finally, a conclusion can be made that a cultural pattern could express itself in corporate behaviour depending on the employee experience, education and skills. Knowing the cultural boundaries of expert recognition and the fundamentals that make an impact on the rationality of decision making, one can adjust an operational research tool (for instance SEJ) according to sector specificity.

Acknowledgement. This project has received funding from European Regional Development Fund (project No. 01.2.2-LMT-K-718-01-0076) under grant agreement with the Research Council of Lithuania (LMTLT).

References

1. Colangelo, E., Kröger, T., Bauernhansl, T.: Substitution and complementation of production management functions with data analytics. Proc. CIRP **72**, 191–196 (2018)
2. Chou, J., Tai, Y., Chang, L.: Predicting the development cost of TFT-LCD manufacturing equipment with artificial intelligence models. Int. J. Prod. Econ. **128**(1), 339–350 (2010). https://doi.org/10.1016/j.ijpe.2010.07.031
3. Elmaraghy, W., Elmaraghy, H., Tomiyama, T., Monostori, L.: Manufacturing technology complexity in engineering design and manufacturing. CIRP Ann. Manuf. Technol. **61**(2), 793–814 (2012). https://doi.org/10.1016/j.cirp.2012.05.001
4. Caputo, A.C., Pelagagge, P.M.: Parametric and neural methods for cost estimation of process vessels. J. Prod. Econ. **112**, 934–954 (2008)
5. Helbig, T., Hoos, J., Westkämper, E.: A method for estimating and evaluating life cycle costs of decentralized component-based automation solutions. Proc. CIRP **17**, 332–337 (2014)
6. Sjöberg, J., Jeppsson, J.: Establishing a cost model when estimating product cost in early design phases, Karlskrona (2017)

7. Mikulskiene, B., Vedluga, T.: Strategies for complexity management coping with cost estimation. The case of customized furniture manufacturing. In: 8th International Conference on Industrial Technology and Management (ICITM), pp. 212–217 (2019). https://doi.org/10.1109/ICITM.2019.8710725

8. Scapolo, F., Miles, I.: Eliciting experts' knowledge: a comparison of two methods. Technol. Forecast. Soc. Chang. **73**(6), 679–704 (2006)

9. de Graaff, M.B., Stoopendaal, A., Leistikow, I.: Transforming clients into experts-by experience: a pilot in client participation in Dutch long-term elderly care homes inspectorate supervision. Health Policy **123**(3), 275–280 (2019)

10. Levallet, N., Chan, Y.E.: Organizational knowledge retention and knowledge loss. J. Knowl. Manage. **23**(1), 176–199 (2019)

11. Blankenship, L., Bruck, T.: Planning for knowledge retention now saves valuable organizational resources later. J. Am. Water Works Assoc. **100**(8), 57–61 (2008)

12. Cooke, R.M., Goossens, L.J.H.: Procedures guide for structured expert judgment. Project Report to the European Commission, EUR, 18820 (1999)

13. French, S.: Aggregating expert judgement. Rev. de la Real Acad. de Ciencias Exactas, Fisicas y Naturales. Serie A. Matematicas **105**(1), 181–206 (2011)

14. Clemen, R.T., Winkler, R.L.: Combining probability distributions from experts in risk analysis. Risk Anal. **19**(2), 187–203 (1999)

15. Cooke, R.M., Goossens, L.L.: TU Delft expert judgment data base. Reliab. Eng. Syst. Saf. **93**(5), 657–674 (2008)

16. Thorne, M.C., Williams, M.M.R.: A review of expert judgment techniques with reference to nuclear safety. Prog. Nucl. Energy **27**(2–3), 83–254 (1992)

17. Simola, K., Pulkkinen, U., Talja, H., Saarenheimo, A., Karjalainen-Roikonen, P.: Comparative study of approaches to estimate pipe break frequencies (No. NKS–79). Nordisk kernesikkerhedsforskning (2002)

18. Peng, W.A., Zan, M.A., Yi, T.I.: Application of expert judgment method in the aircraft wiring risk assessment. Proc. Eng. **17**, 440–445 (2011)

19. Nunes, A., Kirlik, A.: An empirical study of calibration in air traffic control expert judgment. In: Proceedings of the Human Factors and Ergonomics Society Annual Meeting, vol. 49, no. 3, pp. 422–426. SAGE Publications (2005)

20. Jørgensen, M.: A review of studies on expert estimation of software development effort. J. Syst. Softw. **70**(1–2), 37–60 (2004)

21. Rush, C., Roy, R.: Expert judgement in cost estimating: modelling the reasoning process. Concurr. Eng. **9**(4), 271–284 (2001)

22. Aspinall, W.: Expert judgment elicitation using the classical model and EXCALIBUR. In: Seventh Session of the Statistics and Risk Assessment Section's International Expert Advisory Group on Risk Modeling: Iterative Risk Assessment Processes for Policy Development Under Conditions of Uncertainty I Emerging Infectious Diseases: Round IV, pp. 1–22 (2008)

23. Sheskin, D.J.: Handbook of Parametric and Nonparametric Statistical Procedures, 5th edn. Chapman & Hall/CRC, Boca Raton (2011)

24. Corder, G.W., Foreman, D.I.: Nonparametric Statistics for Non-Statisticians. Wiley, Hoboken (2009)

25. Ababei, D.: Excalibur. http://www.lighttwist.net/wp/excalibur. Accessed 02 June 2019

26. Jaiswal, K.S., Aspinall, W., Perkins, D., Wald, D., Porter, K.A.: Use of expert judgment elicitation to estimate seismic vulnerability of selected building types. In: 15th World Conference on Earthquake Engineering (WCEE), pp. 24–28, Lisbon, Portugal, September 2012

27. Kurasova, O., Marcinkevičius, V., Medvedev, V., Mikulskienė, B.: Early cost estimation in customized furniture manufacturing using machine learning. In: Communications in Computer and Information Science. Springer (2019, submitted)
28. Burgman, M., et al.: Redefining expertise and improving ecological judgment. Conserv. Lett. 4(2), 81–87 (2011)

Towards Conceptually Novel Oscillating Agent-Based Simulation of the Relationship Between Cultural Participation and Social Capital

Rimvydas Laužikas[1(✉)] and Darius Plikynas[2]

[1] Faculty of Communication, Vilnius University, Vilnius, Lithuania
rimvydas.lauzikas@kf.vu.lt
[2] Institute of Data Science and Digital Technologies,
Faculty of Mathematics and Informatics, Vilnius University, Vilnius, Lithuania
darius.plikynas@mii.vu.lt

Abstract. Effective simulation and prediction of the social impact of culture is one of the most important questions in contemporary social science and formative cultural policy. After a comprehensive review of the current simulation approaches, we found an evident lack of systematic conceptual models, however. It gave an impetus to investigate some novel conceptual approaches. In general, we admit that cultural events take part in the formation of social capital via the ability to communicate behavioral information in social networks. Following the bottom-up approach, implications of the social impact of cultural events are taking place on the individual (agent or actor) level first. Consequently, the aggregated effect can be simulated and predicted for the group or society (multiagent) level as well. For several reasons, we used CIDOC-CRM cultural ontology, which gives a structured framework of main cultural entities. We discovered that relations between them are not trivial and require fundamentally different viewpoints and simulation frameworks, which would better conform to the emergent complexity of social networks. For this reason, we analyzed in more detail Youri Lotman's semiosphere concept and OSIMAS (an oscillations-based multiagent system) paradigm. Consequently, in the proposed agent-based conceptual model, there is employed not only classical pair-to-pair based Axelrod's neighborhood interaction model but also a one-to-many information broadcasting model. Such conceptual approach is able to provide simulation models for the complex emergent relations between cultural participation and social capital.

Keywords: Cultural participation · Social capital · OSIMAS · CIDOC-CRM · Conceptual model

1 Introduction

Cultural processes are defined as complex dynamic structures of a systematic nature (Lyman 2007). They can be analyzed in contexts of various sciences: philosophy, culture, anthropology, psychology, communication and information, political science

© Springer Nature Switzerland AG 2019
N. Agarwal et al. (Eds.): MSBC 2019, CCIS 1079, pp. 126–144, 2019.
https://doi.org/10.1007/978-3-030-29862-3_10

(Kroeber et al. 1952). Equally, in the various contexts of theoretical and different fields of science, the impact of cultural events, products and services on personal and social change is under consideration (Fujiwara et al. 2014; Hill et al. 2008; Stanley 2006; Taylor et al. 2015).

In analysing the processes of cultural impact on society, the impact of cultural participation on social capital (including social cohesion) is one of the processes that is especially important for the development of society (Armbrecht 2014; Galloway 2009; Partal and Dunphy 2016). Common cultural experiences (as a kind of communicative practice) act as a 'social glue', making society resistant to challenges and mutagenic factors, such as 'linkages between the quality of social capital and a society's ability to discover and implement sustainable development, including a better range of solutions to conflicts over competing uses for natural, social and human resources' (Helliwell et al. 2014). The level of social capital also is an important indicator in quality-of-life measurements (Rogers et al. 2011; Engbers et al. 2017).

However, the researchers who explore the relationship between cultural participation and social capital notice a clear correlation between these two groups of variables. This is particularly striking in relationships between participation in cultural groups and civic behavior, participation in cultural events and trust in institutions, membership in cultural groups and interpersonal trust. And these correlations are more pronounced in the community than at the individual level. However, these correlations (by themselves) do not show a causal relationship (Delaney et al. 2005; Torjman 2004). Thus, the development of methods for establishing a reasonable relationship between participation in cultural events and social capital (and also social capital related social cohesion) is a major challenge for this kind of research. Thus studies on relationship between cultural participation and social capital are important for evidence based cultural impact assessment, rational strategic planning and public policy interventions, including the use of public funds for culture, cultural industries, and creativity.

The paper is developed as part of the project "Social Impact of Cultural Processes: Development of Metrics, Conceptual and Simulation Model". The main goal of research is development of measuring metrics and a conceptual and agent-based simulation models aimed the investigation of the social impact of cultural processes. This paper aims to consider the problem of communicative sharing of social capital through cultural participation, offering the conceptual model of the social impact of dynamic cultural processes as interaction of actors and events. The purpose of the conceptual model is to understand reality-based, social capital construction/ deconstruction through cultural events impact, and to provide simulation models for the complex emergent relations between cultural participation and social capital.

The article uses the CIDOC-CRM terminology. The most important terms of CIDOC-CRM are also semantically related to the terminology used by ABM (Agent Based Modeling). For instance, CIDOC-CRM actors can be interpreted as agents in the MAS terminology.

The conceptual model limitations presented in this article, are as follows: the impact of public and mass cultural events (concerts, etc.) on the actor is investigated, but not the effect of individual events (such as creating a poem, publishing or reading a book, etc.); the study examines the effects of cultural events (via viewing, participation), but does not investigate creative effects of the events on developers and co-authors; the conceptual simulation model deals with the interaction between real-life cultural events and actors (agents) without taking into consideration the events posted on social networks. These limitations are mostly due to the evidence-based restrictions of the employed metrics and feasibility of empirical modelling of simulated processes.

This article is organised as follows: the first chapter discusses the conceptual model (methods, entities and variables) used for explanation of the processes and mechanisms involved in the relationship between cultural participation and social capital. The next two chapters are devoted to discussion of the possibility of applying the Y. Lotman's semiosphere and the OSIMAS (an oscillations-based multi-agent system) paradygm to provide a more precise explanation of the processes of sharing of social capital through cultural participation. Lotman's conceptual schema can be used for the theoretical elaboration of the structures and relationships connecting cultural participation and social capital. Meanwhile, OSIMAS can provide a conceptual means to simulate and investigate various complex and dynamic processes.

2 Conceptual Model

2.1 Methodology

Conceptual modelling is applied to capture relevant aspects of the research topic and for understanding how cultural participation and social capital are related. In our research, we understand "conceptual model" as "an abstract representation of something generalized from particular instances" (Borah 2002) as "a simplified representation of real system" (Liu et al. 2011). It works as "a kind of proto-theory <…> which can then be tested for validity [and] can often help in working through one's thinking about a subject of interest" (Bates 2009). On a methodological level, this conceptual model is created using the CIDOC-CRM methodology. According CIDOC-CRM, a conceptual model consists of two categories of informational elements: (i) classes, describing the concept for an entity, as 'categories of items that share one or more common traits serving as criteria to identify the items belonging to the class' and (ii) properties describing the concept for a process that 'serves to define a relationship of a specific kind between two classes' (Le Boeuf et al. 2015). In this research both elements are derived from the results of a systematic literature review and meta-analysis (performed by authors). The conceptual model was developed as a formal ontological specification of a conceptualisation that is amenable to understanding the relationship between cultural participation and social capital.

For a standardized description of the conceptual model we use generally accepted MAS (multi-agent system) ODD protocol (Grimm et al. 2005; Grimm et al. 2010). This protocol consists of three blocks (Overview, Design concepts, and Details), which are subdivided into seven elements: Purpose, State variables and scales, Process overview and scheduling, Design concepts, Initialization, Input, and Sub models. In the sequence, for conceptual modelling we use Overview block.

2.2 Entities

Based on the theoretical considerations, the social impact of cultural processes is understood as a systemic, targeted process, that can be estimated via dynamics of the social capital. In the course of cultural events, the added value of social capital is created, which generates the social impact of cultural processes. The entities, variables and relationships pertaining to the cultural processes are illustrated in Fig. 1.

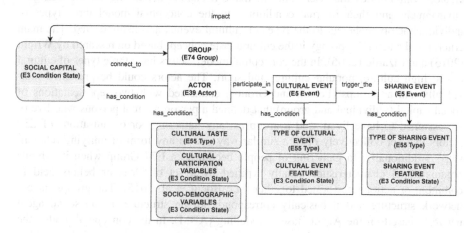

Fig. 1. Entities, variables, and relationships of the model of cultural process.

In the conceptual model, three basic level cultural process entities are distinguished and formalised as CIDOC-CRM classes: individual actors (CIDOC-CRM, E39 Actor), cultural events (CIDOC-CRM, E5 Event) and sharing actions (CIDOC-CRM, E7 Action). A cultural event is perceived as a temporary entity that 'comprises changes of states in cultural, social or physical systems, regardless of scale, brought about by a series or group of coherent physical, cultural, technological or legal phenomena' (Le Boeuf et al. 2015). The concept of 'cultural' can be analysed in various contexts (Kroeber and Kluckhohn 1952). For this research, 'cultural' is understood in a narrower sense as a set of agents' individual attributes that are subject to social influence (Axelrod 1997) and actions performed by agents within cultural domains that are 'a set of practices, activities or cultural products centred around a group of expressions recognised as artistic'. The ESSnet-CULTURE final report lists heritage, archives, libraries, book & press, visuals arts, performing arts, audio-visual & multimedia, architecture, advertising and art crafts (Bina et al. 2012). In the conceptual model, the cultural domains could be generalised as three types of cultural events: high culture, popular culture and sport. The concept of high and popular cultures is based on Pierre Bourdieu's theoretical framework that links different 'cultures' with the theoretical concept of cultural capital (Bourdieu 1986). Meanwhile, sport as a separate event type is defined as 'an activity involving physical exertion and skill in which an individual or team competes against another or others for entertainment' (Sport 2019). Sport as a cultural practice was introduced on the basis of (i) widespread public administration practices that institutionally and temporarily link culture and sport (e.g., UNESCO theme 'Sport') and (ii) the significant impact of sport events on the public in the context of the social capital formation (Taylor et al. 2015).

The actors are defined as 'people, either individually or in groups, who have the potential to perform intentional actions of kinds for which someone may be held responsible' (Le Boeuf et al. 2015). These actors were perceived as adaptive intelligent agents that had an objective, interacted with the environment and with each other and created communities that were able to make decisions depending on the changing environment and their internal conditions. In the conceptual model three types of individual actors, coherent to the types of cultural events, are distinguished. The main criteria of the actors' typology is the cultural taste concept based on research by Wright (2015) and Lizardo (2006). In the conceptual model, actors have three types of cultural tastes: high culture, popular culture, and sport. The actors could be presented individually and as groups (Person and Groups) connected with two representations of social capital (individual and group) that defined a person as 'real persons who live or are assumed to have lived' and a group as 'any gatherings or organisations of E39 Actors that act collectively or in a similar way due to any form of unifying relationship'. Additionally, 'a gathering of people becomes an E74 Group when it exhibits organisational characteristics usually typified by a set of ideas or beliefs held in common, or actions performed together' (Le Boeuf et al. 2015). The groups have a network structure and it basically corresponds to the structure of the social agent network, based on the Agent Based Modelling (ABM). In the conceptual model, the interaction among groups is based on several spatiotemporal patterns: it falls within (contains), in which all members of one (smaller) group are also members of the another (larger) group; it overlaps with, when a part of members of one group is at the same time members of another group; it is separated from, when none member of one group is a member of another group (Le Boeuf et al. 2015).

The third class of entities at conceptual model is the sharing actions, in which one actors share the social capital with another. A sharing actions are 'actions intentionally carried out by instances of E39 Actor that result in changes of state in the cultural, social, or physical systems' (Le Boeuf et al. 2015). In the conceptual model, sharing actions have two types of interactions: the participation in the broadcasted cultural events or by neighborhood interaction among agents. In the context of the OECD model, this sharing should be treated as "social network support" (Scrivens et al. 2013).

2.3   Variables

In the conceptual model every entity (actor, cultural event and sharing action) is described via variables (CIDOC-CRM, E3 Condition state). According to R. Axelrod, these variables describe features or dimensions. For each feature there is a set of traits that are alternative values the feature may have. This abstract formulation means that two individuals have the same culture if they have the same traits of features. The formulation allows us to define the degree of cultural similarity between two individuals as the percentage of their features that have the identical trait pattern (Axelrod 1997).

Individual actors in the model are described using constant (sociodemographic) and dynamical (cultural participation and social capital) variables. In the case of our conceptual model, constant variables are quite common demographic variables: gender, age, education, gaining and location (living place). These variables are important (in correlation with cultural taste) in determining agent involvement in the cultural event.

The dynamic variables correspond to the frequency of participation at cultural events and the four forms of social capital outlined in the OECD scheme (Scrivens et al. 2013). Cultural participation is defined using UNESCO's cultural statistics handbook as 'participation in any activity that, for individuals, represents a way of increasing their own cultural and informational capacity and capital, which helps define their identity, and/or allows for personal expression' (Ellis et al. 2012). In the case of this research, this definition is described in a more detailed form using the CIDOC-CRM as people's participation in a cultural events that alters 'states in cultural, social or physical systems' (in this study's case—resulting in changes in social capital) (Le Boeuf et al. 2015). The variables and values of the measurement of cultural participation is derived from the ESSnet-CULTURE methodology (Bina et al. 2012).

This study's definition and measurement of social capital adopts to the Organisation for Economic Cooperation and Development's (OECD) definition as 'networks together with shared norms, values and understandings that facilitate cooperation within or among groups'. The definition includes the OECD's proposed four distinct interpretations of social capital: Personal relationships, Social network support, Civic engagement, and Trust and cooperative norms (Scrivens and Smith 2013).

Each cultural event is described using sets of features which influence the choice and impact of the cultural event. The important choice features include price, event time, event place, popularity of a creator, and efficiency of advertising. In the conceptual model, these cultural event variables are constant along with the individual agent constant variables that determine his preferences to participate in a particular type of cultural event. The cultural event impact features are event span, frequency, number of spectators and number of performers. In the conceptual model, these are variables that enhance or weaken the impact of a cultural event on the individual and the public.

Each sharing action is described using two features (variables) - temporal and intensity. The temporal variable means that the sharing action happens over a limited extent of time: the duration (time span) from beginning to the end. In our model the sharing actions are perceived as contiguous (without gaps) whereas intensity means the relative level of interactions among individuals in sharing of social capital values. It is important to note that social capital is different from other forms of capital (Robison et al. 2002). Unlike some other forms of capital (with both private and collective benefits), social capital does not decrease when sharing. However, the potential effect of 'satiation' with social capital is possible; social capital is not additive, so its values do not change linearly. In this case, despite the intensive sharing of social capital, the individual's or group's social capital values no longer increase. It can be said that the process of sharing social capital through its mechanisms is closer to the process of sharing other non-material goods (e.g., information) than sharing financial capital. In the conceptual model the sharing of social capital is realised as not less than two types interaction: by participating in broadcasted cultural events and by means of a neighbourhood of a network of actors). These interactions differ in duration and functional mechanisms. Broadcasting as an interaction is shorter, performed during the event in a time span equal to the cultural event, when one actor communicates and shares social capital with others, thus changing the social capital values for both sides. Meanwhile, actors who are not participating in the event can change values of their social capital only through communicating in neighbourhood networks with the agents who participated in the event. In comparison, broadcasting has a much faster and stronger effect than sharing through neighbourhood interactions (longer, less intensive and functionally a reduction in time). It should also be noted that the implementation of a neighbourhood network is twofold: (i) actors who tend to interact with another actors similar to them (a neighbourhood based on cultural similarity; this type of neighbourhood is not fixed) and (ii) actors who tend to interact with another actors who are physically close to them (a neighbourhood based on a physical network; this type of neighbourhood is fixed).

3   Conceptual Model Design Using Semiosphere and Pervasive Information Field Approaches

Review of the related literature has revealed that the core process of social capital formation depends on shared actions that promote communication of behavioral information. Traditional communication and information network research methods can be applied for modeling such processes. However, these methods are general and have to be specifically tailored to model emergent complex social phenomena like social capital dynamics. It is essential to apply these methods in a suitable conceptual framework, however.

There are very few research papers dealing with quantitative modeling or agent-based simulations in this research domain. It can be associated with the complexity and lack of quantitative analytic approaches. Difficulties stem from the lack of (i) suitable quantification methods, (ii) meaningful measuring metrics, and (iii) causal relationship between cultural participation and social capital.

The current research methodology is mostly limited to a disparate survey analysis of cultural participation and social capital estimates over large populations. Such investigations can lead to the correlation estimates, but do not explain causal relations. Besides, they do not strive to model how empirically observed social phenomena can emerge from the bottom-up interactions between agents.

Therefore, we propose a broader conceptual research framework aimed at the extension of the current understanding. It gives some new insights and tools for the quantitative metrics and bottom-up agent-based modeling. In this regard, we propose a framework of two mutually well-matching theories, i.e., semiosphere theory, initially developed by Lotman (2001) and OSIMAS (an oscillations-based multi-agent system) paradigm proposed by Darius Plikynas (Plikynas 2016), see Fig. 2 (illustration A). The figure also depicts the main object of investigation, i.e. modeling of cultural participation impact to social capital.

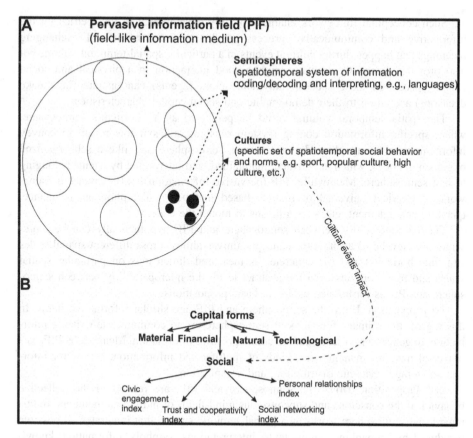

Fig. 2. General scheme of the conceptual model design. Illustration A depicts PIF, semiospheres, and cultures. Illustration B relates cultural events impact to the formation of social capital.

Lotman's conceptual schema can be used for the theoretical elaboration of the structures and relationships connecting cultural participation and social capital. Meanwhile, OSIMAS (an oscillations-based multi-agent system) paradigm can provide a conceptual means to simulate and investigate various complex and dynamic processes (e.g., clustering, cohesion, radicalization, marginalization, etc.) taking place in social mediums (Plikynas 2016; Plikynas and Raudys 2015). The application of OSIMAS paradigm as the theoretical framework provides the means to model a social information network as a pervasive information field (PIF), where each network node (agent) receives pervasive (broadcasted) information-field values. Such an approach is targeted to enforce indirect and uncoupled (contextual) interactions among agents to represent broadcasted cultural information in a form locally accessible and immediately usable by network agents. Therefore, the social system can be modeled as a pervasive information field, where each social information network node receives pervasive information-field values (Plikynas et al. 2015).

Such conceptual framework enables not only development of the metrics for the informative and communicative process of sharing information and exchanging meanings that happen during cultural events in a particular spatial-temporal volume but also provides means to simulate neighborhood interaction in a physical and social capital spaces. In these spaces, individual actors (agents) can operate (i.e., make decisions) according to their demographic and social capital characteristics.

The spatial-temporal volume could be perceived as Y. Lotman's semiosphere, where specific information coding (system of signs and symbols meant to convey information) is taking place. In some sense, semiosphere acts like a self-organized organism of codes, which are created, maintained, and interpreted by agents belonging to that semiosphere. Meanwhile, PIF (pervasive information field) provides a framework of physical universal oscillations-based methods - like phonons, resonance, quantum entanglement, etc. - as a means to model the code.

The interoperability between semiosphere and PIF hypothetically can be represented into levels: (i) abstract (as concepts, universalities across different spatial scales and time horizons) and (ii) concrete (as measured dimensions on particular spatial scales and time horizons). On the abstract level, the interoperability between semiosphere and PIF is formulated using six basic propositions:

1st Proposition. Both, the semiosphere and PIF, are similar informative items. In this regard, the primary functions of semiosphere are to communicate existing information, to generate new information, and to preserve information. Meanwhile, PIF, as a universal medium managing all kinds of multifaceted information, serves for information storage, dynamic distribution, and organization.

2nd Proposition. Both, the semiosphere and PIF, are related to the collective behavior of the conscious and subconscious mind-fields of individual members. In this regard, the semiosphere works as a global semiotic system that integrates all possible (produced by humankind) signs, texts, interpretations, symbols, information, knowledge, representations, and their relationships, including their interaction with the non-semiotic elements from outside of the semiosphere. Meanwhile, PIF, serves as a medium for a collective mind-field of self-organized social level, with the inheritance of some degree of coherent (synchronized) field-like behavior.

3rd Proposition. Both, the semiosphere and PIF, function through information sharing. The information sharing in semiosphere is based on a semiotic presumption about "signs reality", when people share not the information in "pure" sense, but coded symbols meant for decoding and interpretation. For instance, text is understood as an orderly system of signs meant for coded communication. Such coded communication system is distinct from other coded communication systems like visual, audio or tactile captions.

It is important to note that, in the context of Yuri Lotman's semiosphere theory, the texts are perceived not as stable reality objects (with permanent and immutable attributes), but - more like a changing function, acting through the creator, audience, context, and other interactions. The members of particular semiosphere become encoders and interpreters at the same time. They have the capacity to broadcast information for other people (using signs, and codes) and to read the signs left by other people (Lotman 2001). Meanwhile, PIF functions as a pervasive information network, where each network node (agent) receives pervasive (broadcasted) information field values. Social information is coded and spread via social network almost at the speed of light via broadcasting telecommunication networks. The individual members of a society can be modeled as information storing, processing, and communicating agents in an information network society. From another perspective, information societies operate through agents, which are complex, multifaceted self-organized information processes composed of mind-fields of quantum field-like processes originating in brains.

4th Proposition. Both, the semiosphere and PIF operate in a spatiotemporal framework. The spatiotemporal synchrony is a prerequisite for effective real-time communication between agents. Semiosphere, being an open system, is constantly evolving and has a kind of "memory mechanism", which preserves the elements of past conditions or their fragments. For PIF the social order, i.e., self-organized and coherent behavior in social systems, is not so much correlated with the particular patterns of agents' actions, but with the synchrony of their mental activity. That synchrony can be compared to the physical model of superposition of weakly coupled oscillators. Synchronicity is involved in the social-binding problem (how information distributed among many agents generates a community). The social binding process can be imagined as a spatiotemporal resonance state. The contextual information there is distributed in fields, and fields although expressing some global information are locally perceived by agents, who are but a self-organizing part of the same PIF (Plikynas et al. 2015).

5th Proposition. Both, the semiosphere and in some sense PIF are multicentered structures with entirely relative centers and peripheries. The concepts of the center and the periphery in semiosphere are depended on particular (chosen by the investigator) observation point of two structures' interaction. Thus, the same semiosphere structural element, at the same time, can be perceived as the center in terms of one interaction and as the periphery in terms of the other interaction. However, in any case, we find the most developed and most structurally organized elements in the centers, where symbolic coding (e.g., languages and texts) system well operates. In the PIF approach, informational fields are operating on the square, rectangular, or other lattices consisting of a set of nodes. Size of the lattice is arbitrary. All resources and agents are distributed only on these nodes. Each particular node represents a point on virtual lattice space, which functions are for discrete time intervals to evaluate incoming fields and produce corresponding spectra representations, and to oscillate at own fixed natural frequency emanating it to the surrounding PIF.

6th Proposition. Actors of both, the semiosphere and PIF, are trended to semiosphere's creolization (Lotman 2001). In semiosphere, the centers are specific "canonical" structures, which almost eliminate the creation of new texts. Meanwhile, the periphery is the most important and (from the research point of view) the most interesting space of structures interactions (according to Yuri Lotman - texts creolization), which generates the major part of new information. These cultural interaction processes remind not a one-way reception, but they are more like multifaceted, pulsating, sign dialogue between the object and the subject (very relatively defined). According to Yuri Lotman, in order that the two different sign systems' cultural semiosphere structures interact, there must be a blurred boundary between "our own" and "foreign" structure, which usually occurs when one (internal) structure "learns" the language of the other (external) structure (Lotman 2001). Meanwhile, PIF proposes a set of universal physical methods for modeling interaction mechanism between agents. For instance, a trade-off between entropy/negentropy, a stylized phonons model for quantification of oscillatory energy, resonance theory for harmonic oscillators, and even quantum entanglement theory, etc. (Plikynas 2016). Primarily PIF serves as a medium for all information encoding using one or another oscillatory framework, stemming from the physical complex oscillatory networks research. In PIF, each agent absorbs incoming wave packets, superposes them (producing unique spectra), and then transmits them to the environment. The center and periphery here can be understood in terms of synchronization patterns of oscillatory phases.

The prospective development of metrics, measurement, and simulation of individual and group-wise interactions using semiosphere and PIF principles is provided in the discussion below.

4   Sharing of Social Capital in the Framework of Coherent Oscillatory Paradigm

Investigation of the implicit oscillatory nature of agents and social mediums in general can reveal some new ways of understanding the periodic and nonperiodic fluctuations taking place in real life. A closer look at the applied social networks research also reveals some related approaches, which deal, in one way or another, with simulations of the field-like information spreading in social networks. For instance, common behaviours spread through dynamic social networks (Zhang and Wu 2011), the spread of behaviour in online social networks (Centola 2010), urban traffic control with coordinating fields (Camurri et al. 2007), mining social networks using wave propagation (Wang et al. 2012), network models of the diffusion of innovations (Valente 1996), oscillations-based simulation of complex social systems (Plikynas 2010; Plikynas et al. 2014), etc.

On the other hand, some perspicacious, biologically-inspired simulation approaches have emerged in the areas of computational (artificial) intelligence, agent-based and multi-agent systems research (Nagpal and Mamei 2004; Raudys 2004). In turn, these advances have laid the foundations for simulation methods oriented towards intelligent, ubiquitous, pervasive, amorphous, organic computing (Poslad 2009; Servat and Drogoul 2002) and field-based coordination research (Bandini et al. 2006; Camurri et al. 2007; De Paoli and Vizzari, 2003; Mamei and Zambonelli 2006).

In this regard, the major insights of this research are derived from the novel Oscillation-Based Multi-Agent System (OSIMAS) social simulation paradigm, which links emerging research domains via coherent oscillation-based representations of the individual agents and society (as a coherent collective agent system) states as well (Plikynas 2016).

The current peer-to-peer based ABS and MAS direct communication approaches have been unable to incorporate this huge amount of indirect (contextual) information. This is due to the associated complexity and intangibility of the informal information, and the lack of a foundational theory that could create a conceptual framework for the incorporation of implicit information in a more natural way. Thus, there is a need to expand the prevailing ABS/MAS conceptual frameworks in such a way that nonlocal (contextual) interaction and the exchange of information could be incorporated. It seems plausible that we could introduce local MAS_L and nonlocal MAS_N, layers of selforganization in the prospective ABS/MAS simulation platforms

$$MAS = (1 - \eta)MAS_L + \eta MAS_N, \tag{1}$$

where $0 \leq \eta \geq 1$ denotes the degree of nonlocality:
$\eta \Rightarrow 0$, then $MAS = MAS_L$,
$\eta \Rightarrow 1$, then $MAS = MAS_N$.

In this way, we expand the concept of the ABS/MAS by adding nonlocal levels of self-organization. Starting with 0, self-organization could be observed (i) at the local single agent level, (ii) on the intermediate scale $0 << 1$, it could be observed in coherent groups and organizations of agents, and (iii) on the global (social continuum) scale (1), it could be observed in large, coherent, societies of agents. It naturally follows from some real life observations, e.g. agents interact locally (interchanging information with neighbours), but are also affected by the nonlocal states of the whole system (e.g. traditions, cultures, fashions, national mentalities, political situations, economical/financial situations, etc.). Here the term 'nonlocality', which we borrowed from quantum physics, could have many social interpretations, but we prefer to understand it as Jung's archetypes of the collective unconscious, which can be thought of as laws of nature in terms of structures of consciousness (Laszlo 1995).

Thus, below following the OSIMAS paradigm and scheme of conceptual model design (see Fig. 2), there are explained some basic principles of social capital sharing through cultural participation. We start from the proposition that order in social systems can be interpreted in terms of social coherence happening through connections, interactions, and communications, which are taking place between individuals (simulated as agents) (Plikynas 2016). For that matter, semiospheres act as coded systems of communication and cultural events act as broadcasted content itself. In this regard, cultural events are interpreted as a form of formative communication, which is capable of influencing simulated agents' behavioral and communication patterns, and correspondingly their social capital too.

The second proposition is to assume that the relation between the flow of cultural events and their impact on the individual and collective social capital as well is too complicated for the top-down analytical description. Therefore, simple agent-based simulation models can be applied for the bottom-up modeling and investigation of emergent and complex social phenomena.

The third proposition concerns a novel (interdisciplinary) way to model (i) cultural information broadcasting, (ii) agents' communication mechanism, and (iii) the agents themselves. In short, we propose to adapt some well-known methods from physics, i.e., coherent oscillating systems approach.

The central idea is about modeling societies as opened semi-coupled systems of agents. Putting mathematical notations aside, an adaptation of the modeling principles from open physical systems of semi-coupled oscillators can be adapted. That is, following our previous research and well-known Axelrod approach (Axelrod 1997), we interpret agents' neighborhood interactions as semi-coupled oscillators' interactions, where agents are represented as a unique spectral composition of oscillations.

Oscillations' interference mechanism can be applied to model such interactions (Plikynas et al. 2015).

Following this line of thought, cultural events can also be modeled as excitatory energy triggers of oscillatory nature. In the long run, such external triggers can influence the coherence level of the system of semi-coupled agents (oscillators). Cultural excitatory triggers can be periodic or aperiodic (chaotic). Different types of cultural events could be represented using different harmonic frequencies. For instance, in our case, we use three types of events - high culture, popular culture, and sport. The same recurrent type of events can be differentiated using various amplitudes and phases.

Agents' neighborhood interactions and broadcasted cultural events impact - as communication processes - employ encoded semiospheric messaging (see the previous chapter).[1] Events' impact to the system of agents can be modeled as inversely proportional or, e.g., inversely proportional to the square of the distance between the event and an agent in Euclidean physical or social capital space (Plikynas et al. 2019).

In summary, there are three major modules involved: (1) oscillating agent model (OAM), which encodes essential agents' properties in spectral terms,[2] (2) wavelike interaction mechanism (WIM), which encodes rules for interaction between agents and between agents with broadcasted cultural events, and above all, there is a pervasive information field (PIF), which serves as a background medium (space web), where all communication is taking place, and information is stored, see Fig. 3.[3] Such parameterization setup is flexible and robust to represent basic properties of agents', their mutual interactions and broadcasted cultural events impact.

Hence, agents' communication in technical terms is realized via a universal medium, i.e., PIF, and is managed by the wave-like interaction mechanism (WIM). We envisage that oscillating agents can be integrated into a common PIF spectrum as individual sets of oscillation bands, which can be described by the oscillating agent model (OAM). This latter model realizes the production rules for the transformation of

---

[1] In semiosphere, the interaction between an agent and broadcasted cultural event leads to a small change of the agent's social capital, see Fig. 2. The same is true for the agents' mutual interactions.

[2] All time dependant state functions of agents' can be mapped to the frequency domain. An agent becomes represented in terms of a unique composition of vibrations (spectra). Instead of time dependant functions we are operating with spectra now. For transition we can employed the Fourier transform, but we may also use some other transformations like Gabor and wavelet, which can be employed too (Benenson et al. 2006).

[3] The study of coordinated models goes beyond computer science in that evolutionary computation, behavioral sciences, social sciences, business management, artificial intelligence, and logistics also somewhat strictly deal with how social agents can properly coordinate with each other and emerge as globally coherent behaviors from local interactions. To the author's knowledge, the close match to the proposed idea is explored by Mamei and Zambonelli in their study "Field-based coordination for pervasive multi-agent systems" (Mamei and Zambonelli 2006). They have been trying to achieve coordination for multi robotic applications by means of the PIF (pervasive information field) approach. This is an example of how engineers are starting to understand that, to construct self-organizing and adaptive systems, it may be more appropriate to focus on the engineering of proper interaction mechanisms for components of the system rather than on the engineering of their overall system architecture.

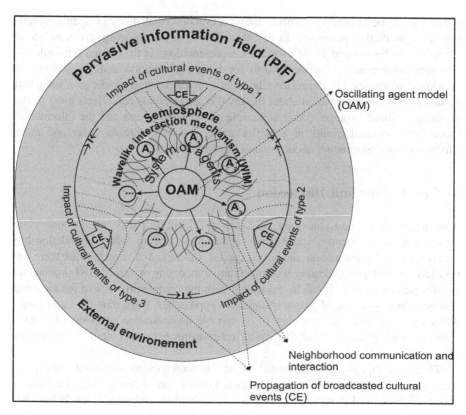

Fig. 3. Sharing of social capital through neighborhood interaction and cultural events impact in the framework of oscillatory paradigm (events and agents emit their characteristic oscillating bands), which is composed of three major modules: oscillating agent model (OAM), wavelike interaction mechanism (WIM), and pervasive information field (PIF). OAM produces a set of oscillating agents {An}, which compose agent-based simulation system. Three investigated types of cultural events (CE) appear in the allotted zones.

internal energy (a set of natural oscillations), which can be defined as a priori or induced from the agents' behavioral strategy.

Two neighboring agents interact if their natural oscillating frequencies and phases coincide. Such interfering interaction can be described using the resonance principle. Admittedly, the resonance increases the oscillating amplitude, i.e., energy, which can be arbitrary transferred to either agent. Such energy sharing can be used to encode social capital sharing. However, the main task of such modeling - to choose the logic for attribution and dynamics of natural frequencies and phases for the agents' population. This task determines the rules of the model and final simulation results (Plikynas 2016).

Members of society (as homeostatic agents) search for ways to sustain and increase self-organized order by increasing internal negentropy. Coordination between agents can be realized through coherent convergence, i.e., the synchronization of oscillation phases. Such social binding involves the synchronous oscillations of agents as self-organized oscillating processes. In this way, having a proper setup, coherent social processes can be reduced to the oscillatory representations in the chosen semiosphere. The semiosphere acts as a mechanism for both – absorption and accelerating of mentioned processes, i.e. the relative boundary of semiosphere works as a filter that passes much more information about its 'own' cultural events and rejects most of the information about 'strange' (other semiospheres) cultural events and the information about 'own' cultural events in a particular semiosfphere spreads faster and more effectively than information about 'strange' cultural events.

5   Conclusions and Discussion

After the review of related literature, we found an evident lack of systematic conceptual models and consequently, quantitative approaches dealing with the relationship between cultural participation and social capital. Investigation revealed that there are very few research papers dealing with quantitative modeling or agent-based simulations in this research domain. It can be associated with the complexity, lack of fundamental understanding, and lack of proper quantitative approaches. Regarding the latter issue, difficulties stem from the drawback of (i) suitable quantification methods, (ii) meaningful measuring metrics, and (iii) causal relationship between cultural participation and social capital.

Therefore, this paper is dedicated for the introduction to the novel conceptual framework in this research domain. It gives not only better understanding of the social impact of dynamical cultural processes on the individual and society levels but also provides some nontraditional insights and tools for the quantitative metrics and bottom-up agent-based modeling.

In this regard, the paper proposes a joint framework of two mutually well-matching theories, i.e., semiosphere theory, initially developed by Yuri Lotman and (Lotman 2001) and pervasive information field (PIF) stemming from OSIMAS (an oscillations-based multi-agent system) paradigm proposed by Darius Plikynas (Plikynas 2016). The interoperability between semiosphere and PIF was investigated and six basic propositions were formulated.

Next, we investigate sharing principles of social capital in the framework of a coherent oscillatory paradigm. A closer look at the applied social networks research also revealed some related approaches, which deal, in one way or another, with simulations of the field-like information spreading in social networks. However, the significant insights of this research are derived from the novel Oscillation-Based Multi-Agent System (OSIMAS) social simulation paradigm, which links emerging research domains via coherent oscillation-based representations of the individual agents and society (as a coherent collective agent system) states as well (Plikynas 2016).

We propose a novel (interdisciplinary) way to model (i) cultural information broadcasting, (ii) agents' communication mechanism, and (iii) the agents themselves. In short, we propose to adapt some well-known methods from physics, i.e., coherent oscillating systems approach. The central idea is about modeling societies as opened semi-coupled systems of agents. We briefly explain how modeling principles from open physical systems of semi-coupled oscillators can be adapted. That is, following our previous research and well-known Axelrod approach (Axelrod 1997), we interpret agents' neighborhood interactions as semi-coupled oscillators' interactions, where agents are represented as a unique spectral composition of oscillations. Oscillations' interference mechanism can be applied to model such interactions (Plikynas et al. 2015). Following this line of thought, cultural events can also be modeled as excitatory energy triggers of oscillatory nature. In the long run, such external triggers can influence the coherence level of the system of semi-coupled agents (oscillators).

In summary, there are three basic modules involved: (1) oscillating agent model (OAM), which encodes essential agents' properties in spectral terms, (2) wavelike interaction mechanism (WIM), which encodes rules for interaction between agents and between agents with broadcasted cultural events, and 3) a pervasive information field (PIF), which serves as a background medium (space web), where all communication is taking place, and information is stored.

Such modeling setup is flexible and robust enough to represent basic properties of agents', their mutual interactions, and broadcasted cultural events impact. It enables expansion of the prevailing ABS/MAS conceptual frameworks in such a way that nonlocal (contextual) interaction and the exchange of broadcasted information could be incorporated naturally.

Just like most studies in the complex social research domain, the proposed conceptual framework requires a thorough further investigation. Additional ABM/MAS based simulation research is necessary to examine, in detail, the issues and criteria that will help to identify the appropriate semiosphere and OAM-WIM-PIF parameter setup to get closer to the simulation of the real-life empirical observations.

Acknowledgement. This research was funded by a grant (No. P-MIP-17-368) from the Research Council of Lithuania.

References

Armbrecht, J.: Developing a scale for measuring the perceived value of cultural institutions. Cult. Trends **23**(4), 252–272 (2014). https://doi.org/10.1080/09548963.2014.912041

Axelrod, R.: The dissemination of culture: a model with local convergence and global polarization. J. Confl. Resolut. **41**(2), 203–226 (1997)

Bandini, S., Manzoni, S., Vizzari, G.: Toward a platform for multi-layered multi-agent situated system (MMASS)-based simulations: focusing on field diffusion. Appl. Artif. Intell. **20**(2–4), 327–351 (2006). https://doi.org/10.1080/08839510500484272

Bates, M.J.: An introduction to metatheories, theories, and models. Libr. Inform. Sci. **11**(4–44), 275–297 (2009)

Benenson, W., Harris, J.W., Stöcker, H., Lutz, H. (eds.): Handbook of Physics. Springer, New York (2006). 1st edn. 2002. Corr. 2nd printing 2006 edn.

Bína, V., et al.: ESSnet-CULTURE European Statistical System Network on Culture. Final report (2012). http://ec.europa.eu/assets/eac/culture/library/reports/ess-net-report_en.pdf. Accessed 14 Apr 2019

Borah, J.J.: Conceptual modeling - the missing link of simulation development. In: Proceedings of Spring Simulation Interoperability Workshop (2002)

Bourdieu, P.: The forms of capital. In: Richardson, J. (ed.) Handbook of Theory and Research for the SOCIOLOGY of Education, pp. 241–258. Greenwood, New York (1986)

Camurri, M., Mamei, M., Zambonelli, F.: Urban traffic control with co-fields. In: Weyns, D., Parunak, H.V.D., Michel, F. (eds.) E4MAS 2006. LNCS (LNAI), vol. 4389, pp. 239–253. Springer, Heidelberg (2007). https://doi.org/10.1007/978-3-540-71103-2_14

Centola, D.: The spread of behavior in an online social network experiment. Science **329**(5996), 1194–1197 (2010). https://doi.org/10.1126/science.1185231

De Paoli, F., Vizzari, G.: Context dependent management of field diffusion: an experimental framework. In: WOA, pp. 78–84 (2003)

Delaney, L., Keaney, E.: Sport and social capital in the United Kingdom: statistical evidence from national and international survey data (2005). http://www.social-capital.net/docs/file/sport%20and%20social%20capital.pdf. Accessed 25 Aug 2018

Ellis, S., Bollo, A., Dal Pozzolo, L., Di Federico, E., Gordon, C.: Measuring cultural participation. Framework for Cultural Statistics Handbook 2 (2012). http://uis.unesco.org/sites/default/files/documents/measuring-cultural-participation-2009-unesco-framework-for-cultural-statistics-handbook-2-2012-en.pdf. Accessed 14 Apr 2019

Engbers, T.A., Thompson, M.F., Slaper, T.F.: Theory and measurement in social capital research. Soc. Indicat. Res. **132**, 537–558 (2017). https://doi.org/10.1007/s11205-016-1299-0

Fujiwara, D., Kudrna, L., Dolan, P.: Quantifying the social impacts of culture and sport (2014). https://www.gov.uk/government/uploads/system/uploads/attachment_data/file/304896/Quantifying_the_Social_Impacts_of_Culture_and_Sport.pdf. Accessed 26 Nov 2018

Galloway, S.: Theory-based evaluation and the social impact of the arts. Cult. Trends **18**, 125–148 (2009). https://doi.org/10.1080/09548960902826143

Grimm, V., Berger, U., DeAngelis, D.L., Polhill, J.G., Giske, J., Railsback, S.F.: The ODD protocol: a review and first update. Ecol. Modell. **221**, 2760–2768 (2010). https://doi.org/10.1016/j.ecolmodel.2010.08.019

Grimm, V., Railsback, S.F.: Individual-Based Modeling and Ecology. Princeton University Press, Princeton (2005)

Helliwell, J.F., Haifang, H., Shun, W.: Social capital and well-being in times of crisis. J. Happiness Stud. **15**, 145–162 (2014). https://doi.org/10.1007/s10902-013-9441-z

Hill, K., Capriotti, K.: Social Effects of Culture: Detailed Statistical Models. Statistical Insights on the Arts, 7:1 (2008). http://www.hillstrategies.com/sites/default/files/Social_effects_models.pdf. Accessed 16 Sept 2018

Kroeber, A.L., Kluckhohn, C.: Culture: A Critical Review of Concepts and Definitions. Peabody Museum of Archaeology and Ethnology, Cambridge (1952). https://archive.org/details/papersofpeabodymvol47no1peab. Accessed 26 Nov 2018

Laszlo, E.: The Interconnected Universe: Conceptual Foundations of Transdisciplinary Unified Theory. World Scientific, Singapore (1995)

Le Boeuf, P., Doerr, M., Ore, C.-E., Stead, S.: Definition of the CIDOC Conceptual Reference Model. Produced by the ICOM/CIDOC Documentation Standards Group, Continued by the CIDOC CRM Special Interest Group. Version 6.2.1 (2015). http://www.cidoc-crm.org/sites/default/files/cidoc_crm_version_6.2.1.pdf. Accessed 26 Nov 2018

Lyman, R.L.: What is the 'process' in cultural process and in processual archaeology? Anthropol. Theory **7**(2), 217–250 (2007). https://doi.org/10.1177/1463499607077299

Liu, J., Yu, Y., Zhang, L., Nie, C.: An overview of conceptual model for simulation and its validation. Proc. Eng. **24**(2011), 152–158 (2011). https://doi.org/10.1016/j.proeng.2011.11.2618

Lizardo, O.: How cultural tastes shape personal networks. Am. Sociol. Rev. **71**(5), 778–807 (2006). https://doi.org/10.1177/000312240607100504

Lotman, Y.: Universe of the Mind: A Semiotic Theory of Culture. I B Tauris & Co Ltd., London (2001)

Mamei, M., Zambonelli, F.: Field-Based Coordination for Pervasive Multiagent Systems. Springer, Heidelberg (2006). https://doi.org/10.1007/3-540-27969-5

Nagpal, R., Mamei, M.: Engineering amorphous computing systems. In: Bergenti, F., Gleizes, M.P., Zambonelli, F. (eds.) Methodologies and Software Engineering for Agent Systems, vol. 11, pp. 303–320. Springer, Boston (2004). https://doi.org/10.1007/1-4020-8058-1_19

Partal and Dunphy (2016)

Plikynas, D., Sakalauskas, L., Laužikas, R., Miliauskas, A., Dulskis, V.: Agent-based simulation of cultural events impact on social capital dynamics. In: IntelliSys2019 Conference Proceedings in the Springer Series Advances in Intelligent Systems and Computing, pp. 1–8 (2019)

Plikynas, D.: A virtual field-based conceptual framework for the simulation of complex social systems. J. Syst. Sci. Complex. 23(2), 232–248 (2010). https://doi.org/10.1007/s11424-010-7239-1

Plikynas, D.: Oscillating agent model: quantum approach. NeuroQuantology. 13(1) (2015)

Plikynas, D.: Introducing the Oscillations Based Paradigm: The Simulation of Agents and Social Systems, p. 325. Springer, Switzerland (2016). https://doi.org/10.1007/978-3-319-39040-6

Plikynas, D., Basinskas, G., Laukaitis, A.: Towards oscillations-based simulation of social systems: a neurodynamic approach. Connect. Sci. 1–24 (2014). http://doi.org/10.1080/09540091.2014.956293

Poslad, S.: Ubiquitous Computing: Smart Devices, Environments and Interactions, 1st edn. Wiley, Chichester (2009)

Raudys, S.: Information transmission concept based model of wave propagation in discrete excitable media. Nonlinear Anal.: Model. Control 9(3), 271–289 (2004)

Robison, L.J., Schmid, A.A., Siles, M.E.: Is social capital really capital? Rev. Soc. Econ. 60(1), 1–21 (2002). https://doi.org/10.1080/00346760110127074

Rogers, S.H., Halstead, J.M., Gardner, K.H., Carlson, C.H.: Examining walkability and social capital as indicators of quality of life at the municipal and neighborhood scales. Appl. Res. Qual. Life 6, 201–213 (2011). https://doi.org/10.1007/s11482-010-9132-4

Scrivens, K., Smith, C.: Four interpretations of social capital: an agenda for measurement. OECD Statistics Working Papers, 2013/06 (2013). http://dx.doi.org/10.1787/5jzbcx010wmt-en

Servat, D., Drogoul, A.: Combining amorphous computing and reactive agent-based systems: a paradigm for pervasive intelligence? In: Proceedings of the First International Joint Conference on Autonomous Agents and Multiagent Systems: Part 1, pp. 441–448. ACM, New York (2002). http://doi.org/10.1145/544741.544842

Sport: English. Oxford Living Dictionary. Oxford University Press, Oxford (2019)

Stanley, D.: The social effects of culture. Can. J. Commun. 31(1), 7–15 (2006). http://www.cjc-online.ca/index.php/journal/article/view/1744/1857. Accessed 26 Nov 2018

Taylor, P., Davies, L., Wells, P., Gilbertson, J., Tayleur, W.: A review of the social impacts of culture and sport (2015). https://www.gov.uk/government/uploads/system/uploads/attachment_data/file/416279/A_review_of_the_Social_Impacts_of_Culture_and_Sport.pdf. Accessed 26 Nov 2018

Torjman, S.: Culture and recreation: links to well-being (2004). https://maytree.com/publications/culture-and-recreation-links-to-well-being/. Accessed 26 Nov 2018

Valente, T.W.: Network models of the diffusion of innovations. Comput. Math. Organ. Theory 2(2), 163–164 (1996). https://doi.org/10.1007/BF00240425

Wang, X., Tao, H., Xie, Z., Yi, D.: Mining social networks using wave propagation. Comput. Math. Organ. Theory 19(4), 569–579 (2012). https://doi.org/10.1007/s10588-012-9142-x

Wright, D.: Understanding Cultural Taste: Sensation, Skill and Sensibility. Palgrave Macmillan, London (2015)

Zhang, Y., Wu, Y.: How behaviors spread in dynamic social networks. Comput. Math. Organ. Theory **18**(4), 419–444 (2011). https://doi.org/10.1007/s10588-011-9105-7

Author Index

Agarwal, Nitin   41
Agieva, M. T.   29
Alassad, Mustafa   41
Ando, Ryosuke   55

Bubeliene, Daiva   12

Gubar, Elena   96

Hussain, Muhammad Nihal   41

Juknevicius, Stanislovas   3

Kleiner, George   68
Koponen, Ismo T.   82
Korolev, A. V.   29
Kumacheva, Suriya   96

Laužikas, Rimvydas   126
Liu, Wei   55

Medvedev, Viktor   112
Merkys, Gediminas   12
Mikulskienė, Birutė   112

Navickienė, Olga   112
Nishihori, Yasuhide   55

Ougolnitsky, G. A.   29

Plikynas, Darius   126

Rybachuk, Maxim   68

Tomilina, Galina   96

Ushakov, Dmitry   68

Vedlūga, Tomas   112

Yang, Jia   55

Zhitkova, Ekaterina   96

Printed in the United States
By Bookmasters